IMAGES
of America

FORT SMITH

On the Cover: FA group of local boys gather for football practice at the Boys Club behind Andrews Field in Fort Smith, Arkansas, in 1940. Pictured are, from left to right, (first row) Charles Danley, Bobby Bell, Pat Garner, Cecil Russell, ? Slaughter, Raymond Vaughn, and C.B. Turnipseed; (second row) Jerry Robinson, Bob "Bobby" Joe Becker, Billy McGinnis, and Billy Vaughn. In the 1950s, Bob Becker played for several semiprofessional baseball teams in the Fort Smith area. (Becker family collection.)

IMAGES
of America

FORT SMITH

Kevin L. Jones

ISBN 9781531668556

Published by Arcadia Publishing
Charleston, South Carolina

Library of Congress Control Number: 2013936589

For all general information, please contact Arcadia Publishing:
Telephone 843-853-2070
Fax 843-853-0044
E-mail sales@arcadiapublishing.com
For customer service and orders:
Toll-Free 1-888-313-2665

Visit us on the Internet at www.arcadiapublishing.com

This work is dedicated to my parents, Doyle and Helen Jones, and the following for their encouragement: Carolyne Jones, Darin Jones, Warren and Cynthia Matlock, Jack and Vanda "Punkie" Hires, Theresa Hires, Charles "Chuck" and Billie Webb, James Loren Janes, Nick and Kim Janes, and of course, my wife, Maggie, and our son, Patrick. This book is also dedicated to my mother-in-law, Ida Lue "Turnip" (née Turnipseed) Janes (1935–2012), and all of her stories about this area.

Contents

Acknowledgments

This work would not have been possible without the patience and encouragement of my wife, Maggie, and our son, Patrick. Additionally, thanks go to Artie Berry, Billie "Trick" Webb, and James Loren Janes; Caroline Speir, Leisa Gramlich, Connie Manning, and the Fort Smith Museum of History; Loren McLane, Jeremy Lynch, and the Fort Smith National Historic Site; Tom Wing, Joe Wing, Greg and Sherry Hall, Dennis and Martha Siler, Bradford Randall, Sherrell Buchanan, Rick Ruth, Steve Sharum, Philip and Andrew McClure, Allison Reeves, Shelia Croxton, Billy Higgins, Bob Becker, Robin Morse, Linoel Baker, Jennifer Baker, Elizabeth Baker, Lisa Neisler, Evangeline Werner, Craig Rivaldo, Joe Wasson, R.D. and Penny Casey, Janie Glover, Susan Krafft, and the Fort Smith Chamber of Commerce; Shelly Blanton and the Pebley Center at the University of Arkansas at Fort Smith, Boreham Library; Sharon Blentlinger and the faculty and staff of Immaculate Conception School, especially the Immaculate Conception cafeteria ladies Dawn Drackett, Janet Haddock, Isidra Kaelin, and Eva Lawson. Thanks also go to Joe Hardin, Cammie Sublette, Paul Beran, and the administration, faculty, and staff of the University of Arkansas at Fort Smith for their support of projects such as this one, and the promotion of local history research.

Introduction

Fort Smith has a rich history. The images in these pages are a small sampling of the numerous photographs available to researchers and the average person who enjoys the past. Fort Smith was once called the "most industrial city in Arkansas." The creative energies and entrepreneurial spirit of past citizens can be seen in these images. Fort Smith's history is an example of what has occurred nationwide since the 1800s. Like many river towns, Fort Smith saw opportunities in its natural resources, its immigrant population, and the push to civilize the West. The influence of the federal government has been felt in Fort Smith since 1817 and continues to help foster economic and cultural development. From the building of the first fort on Belle Pointe to the era of Judge Isaac C. Parker and the US marshals, Fort Smith was a hard place to live. The federal court and local law enforcement helped tame, to a degree, the area's lawlessness, and mixed with technological and social changes of the era, Fort Smith began to be a center for business and culture. The period between Reconstruction and the Great Depression was a time of progress and refinement for the area. World War II would affect Fort Smith by bringing the federal government back by establishing Fort Chaffee and the Air National Guard in the 1940s and 1950s.

The post-war era of Fort Smith mirrored the development of similar-sized towns in the mid-South and Midwest. Mining, farming, and making furniture put Fort Smith on the map. Many nationally known companies opened factories and distribution centers here after World War II. As the nation has endured booms and busts, recessions have also hit Fort Smith, but these images show a resilient population that refuses to be counted out. As manufacturing has waxed and waned, the medical industry and academics have become a catalyst for a more stable economy.

Several areas of the town that were previously not well known or were forgotten are showcased in this book. Neighborhoods such as Southtown and Massard are introduced, and the important businesses and cultural contributions that have happened over the years are also reviewed briefly. Those who know the stories from firsthand accounts are dwindling in number, and the time to write the stories down is passing. We are liable to lose history of certain areas and peoples, and so, attention must be paid to the people, places, and events of the past before it is too late. This book hopes to capture some of the area's stories through images.

One

Rebels in Fort Smith, Hell on the Border, and Respectability

According to the Titchenal family history, this 1853 lithograph of Fort Smith shows the 1823 homestead of blacksmith John R. and Rebecca (Harbert) Tichenal, near the 1838 commissary building. The small, dark structure at center symbolizes the birthplace of Sarah Ann Titchenal, born December 23, 1823. A marker to Sarah Ann naming her "the first white child born in Fort Smith" is near the commissary building at the Fort Smith National Historic Site. The Noon Civics Club, one of the city's oldest organizations, established this marker in 1936. The date on the marker is incorrect, and the spelling on the marker is shown as "Tichnell." Sarah Ann married Jeremiah Hackett Jr. in 1841. Jeremiah Hackett Jr. served with the 2nd Arkansas Cavalry as captain and major in Company H and was in the Arkansas legislature. The family also established Hackett, Arkansas, south of Fort Smith. Jeremiah Hackett Jr.'s Irish immigrant grandfather Thomas Hackett Jr. served in the American Revolution and settled in Maryland. (Fort Smith Museum of History.)

Charles A. Birnie Sr., an early Fort Smith resident and tinner, built this home at Washington (now Second) Street in 1846. Charles Jr. learned his father's trade, served in the Confederate army, and moved to California in 1864. After Charles Jr.'s stint in the army and out West, he returned to Fort Smith to paint the neglected government buildings and later opened a furniture and coffin company with his uncle George and brother H.C. Birnie. (Fort Smith Museum of History.)

Built between 1865 and 1870, this home is an example of a family doing better than average as it recovered from the recent hostilities. The War Between the States ravaged Arkansas natives, and homes, such as this one, rose from the ashes of that terrible era. This original structure was located at the northwest corner of North Ninth and C Streets. (Fort Smith Museum of History.)

This photograph is assumed to be the corral and stable area of the second Fort Smith around the time of the Civil War. Many large homes and established stores were near the fort, as it served as a hub of commerce and traffic. (Fort Smith Museum of History.)

This early 1900s postcard, looking west, reveals a more accurate view of the second Fort Smith than earlier lithographs. Demolished in the mid-20th century, the quartermaster's building is seen to the south (at far left); the commissary building to the north (far right), which, for a time, served as Judge Isaac C. Parker's office, is obscured by trees. The structures of the second Fort Smith evolved after the US Army left in the 1870s. One of two officer's quarters burned while the remaining one (at right) became the federal courthouse and jail for the Western District for Arkansas and Indian Territory from the 1870s through the 1890s. The jail at left was constructed in the 1880s due to the conditions of the "Hell on the Border" basement jail. (Fort Smith Museum of History.)

This 1860s view from the second fort shows Garrison Avenue and the Arkansas River. Federals abandoned the fort in 1861 while Confederates stayed until 1863. Both armies left with little action due to food scarcity, as bushwhackers and local actions destroyed supply lines. Rebel artillery later fired from across the river, causing trees to be cut and a trench to be dug to current Dodson Avenue and Old Greenwood Road. Pvt. Henry Strong of Company K, 12th Kansas Infantry, describes "fatigue duty" in his 1860s diary *A Rough Introduction to This Sunny Land*, edited by Tom Wing, and details all local "able-bodied men and boys" building trenches, blockhouses, and four firing platforms in February 1864. (Fort Smith Museum of History.)

The 1st Arkansas (Union) Light Artillery is shown after Massard Prairie and Devil's Backbone (1863–1865). George Maledon, the "Prince of Hangmen" for Judge Parker, was a German immigrant who came to Fort Smith at 18, became a police officer, and joined the 1st Arkansas. Solomon Hires (also with the 1st Arkansas) later moved to Taney County, Missouri. William Jackson Smart, born in Fort Smith (1842), served with the 1st Arkansas, and his daughter, Sonora Louise Dodd, established Father's Day. (Cynthia Williams collection.)

Written on this photograph is: "Garrison Avenue 1860. Union refugees drawing veterans. Not one dollar in the crowd." Henry Strong's 1860s diary notes Union soldiers earned $12 a month. Duty was difficult for both sides, and the natives suffered. Northwest Arkansas, Indian Territory, and the river valley were in federal control after the battles of Prairie Grove, Pea Ridge, and Honey Springs, and the actions at Massard Prairie and Devil's Backbone. Southern sympathies returned during Reconstruction. (Fort Smith Museum of History.)

W.R. Dodson once lived in Jenny Lind, Arkansas. This photograph, taken in Los Angeles, depicts a private of Company G of the 9th Missouri (Confederate). A 1900 census shows an El Monte, Los Angeles, address, and a California grave details William Riley Dodson (1839–1921) as a private of Company B of Harrell's Battalion Arkansas Cavalry (CSA). The 9th Missouri "Buster's battalion" (also known as "Benton's battalion") became the 15th Battalion Arkansas Cavalry and fought at Prairie Grove, Pleasant Hill, Jenkins Ferry, and Indian Territory. It is unknown whether "W.R." is related to John Dodson, an Irish immigrant who gave his textile fortune to the Confederate war effort and later to Fort Smith Irish and German immigrants. (Fort Smith Museum of History.)

Col. E.C. Boudinot, Cherokee lawyer and statesman, is shown in this 1860s portrait taken at 114 Garrison Avenue in R.G. Bulgin's studio. The Oklahoma Historical Society's *Encyclopedia of Oklahoma History and Culture* states that Elias Cornelius (1835–1890) was born in Georgia. His father, Elias, was assassinated for promoting the Treaty of New Echota. The younger Elias was educated in New England and moved west. He edited newspapers and practiced law in Fayetteville and Little Rock, Arkansas. Boudinot was secretary of Arkansas's secession and joined his uncle, Gen. Stand Watie, in many battles and skirmishes. Later, he argued at the US Supreme Court regarding Cherokee rights and individual land ownership. He was instrumental in naming Oklahoma state, promoted "boomers," founded Vinita, Oklahoma, and practiced law in Fort Smith at the time of his death in 1890. His uncle was the last Confederate general to surrender. (Fort Smith Museum of History.)

Sgt. H.B. Hale had his picture taken in Cook's Studio at 708 Garrison Avenue in Fort Smith. Hale lived for a time in Cedar Creek, Arkansas (now Devil's Den State Park). He served as a Crawford County judge from 1880 to 1882 and also in 1886. (Fort Smith Museum of History.)

According to the *Southwest Times Record*, in September 1903, hundreds gathered for the dedication of a memorial to the Confederate war dead in Fort Smith. US senator James H. Berry and military officials, as well as many Confederate veterans (some dressed in their gray uniforms or carrying equipment and flags), attended the gathering. (Fort Smith Museum of History.)

Brig. Gen. William L. Cabell (middle, with cane) is shown with Confederate veterans memorializing Fort Smith's war dead. Cabell served at Jefferson Barracks in Missouri; Fort Gibson, Indian Territory; and Fort Smith as a quartermaster in the US Army before the Civil War. As a Confederate brigadier general, Cabell fought at Pea Ridge, Devil's Backbone, and Price's Raid, among others. A Virginian by birth, he returned to Fort Smith after the war, worked as a civil engineer, and studied law. He was admitted to the Arkansas Bar in 1868. He left for Texas in 1872. He served as mayor of Dallas, Texas (1874–1882); US marshal for the Northern District of Texas (1885–1889), and the vice president of Trunk Railroad. He established the Austin, Texas, home for Confederate veterans. Cabell died in 1911 at age 84. (Fort Smith Museum of History.)

Pictured in 1898, members of the "Kettle Drum" are, from left to right, (first row) Mrs. Alf Williams, Mrs. Harvey C. Read, Mrs. Carter, Mrs. Joe Williams, and Mrs. James Read; (second row) Mrs. Locke, Mrs. C.E. Speer, Mrs. Halloway, Mrs. Sloan, and Mrs. Eugene Heudersous. They were part of the United Daughters of the Confederacy who raised $2,332.39 through parties, booth sales, and donations for a monument to Gens. A.E. Steen and James McIntosh (CSA), buried in the Fort Smith National Cemetery. Steen died at Prairie Grove, and McIntosh died at Pea Ridge in 1862. The original marker was destroyed by the 1898 cyclone, the second marker was too small, and a 1903 statue was made more elaborate. The quartermaster general of the Army and US secretary of war Elihu Root objected to the monument in the cemetery for being too pro-Southern. Citizens brought the marker to Fort Smith's Sebastian County Courthouse grounds, where it stands today. (Fort Smith Museum of History, Archives and Special Collections, University of Arkansas, Little Rock.)

This 1890s–1910s photograph from Wynoma Day of Talequah, Oklahoma, shows a Union veteran who appears to have "seen the elephant," meaning that he has combat experience. His expression and weapon suggest an eventful history. (Fort Smith Museum of History.)

This photograph reveals the typical landscape and people of the Fort Smith area during Reconstruction. (Fort Smith Chamber of Commerce.)

This photograph shows the alley between Fifth and Sixth Streets to Sixth and Garrison Avenue in downtown Fort Smith in the 1870s. "Reutzel" is a name found today in the area. Henry Reutzel, born in 1846 in Germany, came to the city in 1848. He served as Union chief clerk in the commissary after 1863, providing for locals and soldiers alike. After the war, he was a leading cotton merchant, and laid the first concrete sidewalk in Fort Smith. After 1887, he led local construction and real estate for a time and later operated a guttering and sidewalk company. He is also responsible for paving Garrison Avenue with bricks. The store at right (possibly Ben Atkinson's) is selling stoves and tinware. (Fort Smith Chamber of Commerce.)

This gathering is following a parade on Garrison Avenue near the Reutzel and Atkinson stores. Pictured are, from left to right, on horseback, Henry I. Falconer Sr., John Rogers, P.R. Davis, and Ben Atkinson. Falconer worked in the Western District of Arkansas and was appointed later in the late 1890s by Chief Marshal J.J. McAlester of Muskogee in the "Sandy Land Court," working out of Muskogee. John H. Rogers, a Confederate war veteran, was twice wounded and received a commission for gallantry as a first lieutenant on the battlefield at age 19 in Franklin, Tennessee. Rogers became a lawyer, judge, and US representative. P.R. Davis was a local grocer, and Benjamin F. Atkinson served as a Confederate captain and colonel in Fort Smith. After the war, he established a hardware store at 623 Garrison Avenue and was president of the American National Bank. (Fort Smith Museum of History.)

Pictured is the old "Red Mill" at Garrison Avenue and Tenth Street around 1869. Included in this group of men are H. Johnson, businessman E.B. Bright, and Judge John F. Wheeler, who published the first Fort Smith newspaper. (UALR Center for Arkansas History and Culture/Fort Smith Museum of History.)

John B. Williams and Leon Williams established the Pony Express Company. Additionally, these men operated the 444 Ranch near Fort Smith. This photograph is unique due to the snow on the ground, as most would not associate snow with Fort Smith, but those who have lived here know that any weather is possible, and a wide divergence of temperatures in a given day is probable. (Fort Smith Museum of History.)

The 444 Pony Express Wagon and Market Company at North Tenth and A Streets was part of the Texas Wagon Yard at Texas Corner in Fort Smith. The owner, John B. Williams, was a friend of Emmett Dalton and served as sheriff from 1929 to 1934. (Fort Smith Museum of History.)

John B. Williams is seen in the office of the 444 Pony Express and Market Company in the early 1900s. The official certificate above the desk is to show that the establishment could send Western Union telegrams and packages. The rules on the wall also remind employees and customers of the business environment Williams wanted. (Fort Smith Museum of History.)

Leon Williams, brother of John B Williams, drives cattle on the 444 Ranch near Fort Smith. John B. Williams was with Andy Carr on March 23, 1912, when they assisted two detectives with Sanford Lewis, an African American who was arguing with a woman on Garrison Avenue. Williams, Carr, and the detectives were breaking up the argument when Lewis ran, encouraging the men to arrest him. During the scuffle and pistol-whipping of Lewis, a gun went off, killing Carr. A lynch mob of over 400 formed later that night, took Lewis out of jail, and hanged him on a trolley pole in front of the Hotel Main and First National Bank of Fort Smith. Williams was later acquitted of involuntary manslaughter in the deaths of Lewis and Carr. (Fort Smith Museum of History.)

Shown are the Cherokee Nation chiefs from 1828 to 1916. W.C. Rogers was living in Skiatook, Indian Territory, when he was charged with selling alcohol to the tribe and with assault. Will Rogers's father, Clement Vann Rogers, posted bail for the assault. In July 1893, W.C. was tried for murdering Deputy US Marshal Lee Taylor, who had an eye for Rogers's wife. At the time of the incident, Lee was apprehending whiskey runners. Rogers claimed self-defense when asked why he shot Taylor. Judge Isaac C. Parker found Rogers not guilty. Rogers died of pneumonia and flu in 1917 at Skiatook, Oklahoma. (Fort Smith Museum of History.)

Sen. Nelson Chigley (1830–1922), shown in this Finkley Studio lithograph, was born in Mississippi and was forced with other Chickasaw tribal members westward. He lived at Fort Coffee, then Blue Creek, and moved to the Washita Valley in 1854. In Davis, Murry County, Indian Territory, he developed the Davis Mining Company. By 1890, he had over 2,000 acres. Chigley, a well-respected leader and Chickasaw senator, was instrumental in tribal politics at the local and national level. He also served briefly as the Chickasaw governor. His home stands today in Davis, Oklahoma. (Fort Smith Museum of History.)

At the Chickasaw capital Tishomingo, Indian Territory, in 1899, are, from left to right, (first row) unidentified and Wyatt Chigley (1878–1939); (second row) George Murry, ex-governor William Guy, Nelson Chigley, and Louis Seelay; (third row) Joe Newberry, George Colbert, Robert Imotiche, and Ruben Carney. Wyatt's daughter Ruby Chigley Lynch is buried at Rose Lawn Cemetery in Fort Smith. This meeting followed the Curtis Act of 1898. (Fort Smith Museum of History.)

The Sebastian County Courthouse/Fort Smith City Courthouse and Offices are at left, and the new federal courthouse is at right on Sixth Street in Fort Smith. The county courthouse (built in the late 1880s) had a height of 148 feet. The clock tower was replaced in 1910. The bell is housed in the Fort Smith Museum of History. This structure was replaced in 1937 by an Art Deco one (also known as a Works Progress Administration Moderne building). The building at right was constructed in 1889–1890, housing the post office and federal courthouse. The Isaac C. Parker Federal Building was erected on the site in 1937 in Classical Revival style. (Fort Smith Museum of History.)

This photograph is the only known one of Judge Isaac C. Parker at the bench in Fort Smith. It was taken inside the new building constructed in 1889–1890 on Sixth Street. Parker used this courthouse for only a short time, as he died in 1896. He tried over 13,000 cases in 21 years, and some say he died of exhaustion, but he was known to have Bright's Disease. Parker was born in Ohio, served Missouri in the US House of Representatives, and was appointed by Pres. Ulysses S. Grant to the federal bench in Fort Smith in 1875 at age 34. He was also influential on Fort Smith school and hospital boards and helped the once-wild community grow into a cultural and economic center. (Fort Smith Museum of History.)

The Fort Smith chapter of the International Brotherhood of Electrical Workers (IBEW) is seen in 1891. Originally known as the Electrical Wiremen and Linemen's Union in St. Louis in 1890, the organization then became the National Brotherhood of Electrical Workers in 1891. Fort Smith's contemporary IBEW Local 700 was chartered in 1937. (Pebley Center, Boreham Library, University of Arkansas at Fort Smith.)

The Grand Opera House (dedicated October 10, 1887, and closed 1910) at South Fifth Street and Garrison Avenue was a massive yellow-brick building designed by Noxen, Albet, and Looney of St. Louis. William H. Byram of Fort Smith supervised construction of the building co-owned by John S. Park, Ben DuVal, and William M. Cravens. George Tilles managed the 1,100-seat theater. Judge John Rogers spoke at the dedication. The Grand Opera House Company foreclosed in 1892. DuVal lost an 1899 case versus the School District of Fort Smith regarding an 1887 loan of $30,000 with the property as mortgage. (Fort Smith Museum of History.)

Postmaster James Brizzolara (right) is seen in the Sixth Street Courthouse and Post Office in the 1890s. Brizzolara, an Italian immigrant, served during the Italian revolution and was mustered out at age 14 as a colonel. The *New York Times* of September 25, 1913, reported that he enjoyed duels and was badly wounded in one with George R. Phelan in Memphis in 1869. A US commissioner for 19 years and mayor of Fort Smith from 1878 to 1882, his home was at Sixth and E Streets. He died in 1913. (Fort Smith National Historic Site.)

Berry-Wright Dry Goods, seen in 1901, was located on the west corner of Third Street and Garrison Avenue. Dallas Yell Berry and Oliver Echols started the store in 1898, adding I.F. Wright in 1899. J. Foster's grocery was also here before Berry. Some suggest a cemetery once existed next to the building, and that a 1936 addition covered it. The building was sold in the 1980s, according to Arthur "Artie" Berry, and those next door were converted into office space, called the 200 Garrison Building. A 1996 tornado destroyed most of the block. After demolition, that half of the block became Pendergraft Park. (Arthur Berry collection.)

Past the Hotel Main is the huge clock tower of the Sebastian County and Fort Smith Courthouse, built in the 1880s on Sixth Street. This photograph was taken prior to 1910. The left portion of the Hotel Main Building was occupied by the National Bank of Western Arkansas, which originated in 1872, but moved to the location pictured here in 1888. The bank evolved into First National Bank of Fort Smith that year. The current white-brick structure at Sixth Street and Garrison Avenue was completed in 1911. (Fort Smith Museum of History.)

Harry G. Barr Company and Goff Grocery, "Where Spending Is A Pleasure" (according to their sign), were located in the old Grand Opera House Building. Barr opened Barr's Building Specialties in 1934, moved to 513 Garrison in 1938, and then into the old Grand Opera House in 1944. The company moved in 1954 to Thirty-second Street and to Zero Street at the current location in 1972. Weather-Barr products are nationally known, yet the company is still family-owned and operated from Fort Smith. (Fort Smith Museum of History.)

This September 22, 1898, view of the Fort Smith Water Works shows families enjoying the fountain and one person near the building holding a guitar. Like many growing cities in this era, Fort Smith had to change with its population and utilize its natural resources or create new ways to bring those resources to its citizens. (Fort Smith Museum of History.)

A group gathers at a cotton gin in Fort Smith around 1900. Cotton was big business, as railroads, river shipping, and early automobiles increased the supply to demanding customers worldwide. Cotton from Fort Smith helped the local banks as well, as they maintained loans to local merchants and cotton growers. (Fort Smith Museum of History.)

Fort Smith Light and Traction Company (FSL&T) was formed from two companies, the Fort Smith Railway Company (began in 1883 with mule-drawn trolleys) and the Fort Smith & Van Buren Electric Street Railway Light and Power Company of 1893. A merger in 1903 created the powerful FSL&T, which lasted until the 1920s. According to the Fort Smith Trolley Museum, business decisions regarding fares, tolls, routes, and arguments with the city about maintenance battered the company. Oklahoma Gas and Electric took over in 1933, changed the name, and ended streetcar service in Fort Smith until private interest from the community restored some of the original cars and lines to run these trolleys once again. For a small fee, anyone can ride the restored cars downtown and visit the interesting Fort Smith Trolley Museum located near the Fort Smith National Cemetery. (Fort Smith Chamber of Commerce.)

These men are in the service area of the Fort Smith Light and Traction Company around 1911. The project before them appears to be streetlamps, as two men are testing sockets, and the others have another waiting beside them. Electric streetlamps began to line Garrison Avenue in the late 1910s, and by 1925, the city was aglow with them on most of the major thoroughfares. (Fort Smith Chamber of Commerce.)

This is a November 1911 photograph of the machine shop within the Fort Smith Light and Traction Company Building; it provides examples of how streetcars may have been retooled and how the linemen may have taken their breaks where their lockers where lined on the wall at right. Grinders and lathes are visible, as are extra trolley car controls and moneyboxes on the shelves at left. The other half of this room contained a wall phone, water cooler, and mailboxes. (Fort Smith Chamber of Commerce.)

The Fort Smith Light and Traction Company's powerhouse is seen in 1911. The interior workings of the generators and main control for power to Fort Smith and the genesis for the popular Fort Smith Light and Traction Company's citywide trolley system were within this building. (Fort Smith Chamber of Commerce.)

This is a 1906 photograph at the Fort Smith Refrigerator Works at South Fifth and E Streets. As innovation ushered in new technologies in the new century, men such as these provided services that are now commonplace, but in 1906, the area was changing from iceboxes to machine-cooled units. Slaughterhouses, grocers, and movie theaters of the early 1920s would benefit from the hard work of these early pioneers in refrigeration techniques and tools. (Fort Smith Museum of History.)

An Atkinson-Williams Hardware employee drives the first truck wagon down the alley between Garrison Avenue and North A Street. Fink's Jewelry store is visible at Seventh Street and Garrison Avenue in background. The Atkinson-Williams hardware building at 320 Rogers Avenue is now home to the Fort Smith Museum of History. (Fort Smith Museum of History.)

The printing office of Weldon, Williams, and Lick shows, around 1903, various methods of print making that had been in use with metal type for decades. Organized by Oliver Weldon, George Williams, and Chauncey Lick in 1898, the company exists today at 711 North A Street and continues to supply the world with tickets, banners, posters, and large and small jobs for corporations and individuals. (Fort Smith Museum of History.)

This man and his helper (in the wagon) are peddling molasses at North B and Tenth Streets in Fort Smith around 1906. (Fort Smith Museum of History.)

Blacksmith John Erman is in his shop at Massard, Arkansas, in the early 20th century. This was an integral part of many communities, as farmers, ranchers, and the average citizen would often require a tool to be fixed, replaced, or made from scratch. The village of Massard (located south of the Arkansas River and Wildcat Mountain and north of what is now Zero Street and the original battlefield of Massard Prairie) was eventually absorbed by Fort Smith as more businesses and residents moved down the highway toward Barling and Fort Chaffee during the 1950s, 1960s, and 1970s. (Rick Ruth collection.)

Fort Smith's Southern Broom Company merged with Dixie Broom from Hope, Arkansas, in 1916. The Southern Broom Company, pictured here in the early 1900s, employed 30 people. Broom production nationally in 1904 was 60 million brooms, according to the *New York Times*. The H.H. Lairamore Broom Company on Hendricks Boulevard continues to make brooms and other cleaning products that are sold internationally. Lairamore began his company in downtown Fort Smith in 1943. He moved the business after the flood of 1943 to where it is today. (Fort Smith Chamber of Commerce.)

Workers pay close attention to the fast-moving flywheel of a steam-driven engine and pulley system at the Southern Broom Company around 1904 in Fort Smith. Workers attach broomcorn threads to handles. Broomcorn hanging from the rafters dries overhead before it is cut and tied to the handles. (Fort Smith Chamber of Commerce.)

The maze of pulleys, bands, and electric wires are mixed with planks, shaping tools, clamps, and finished products in this chair factory in Fort Smith in the early 1900s. The area was once a leader in furniture construction and distribution. The abundant natural resources and transportation around Fort Smith helped maintain its influence. Few companies, including Riverside Furniture (since 1947) and Eads Brothers (since 1901), remain in the once-thriving local industry. (Fort Smith Chamber of Commerce.)

Fred G. Hicken's Cigars and Tobacco and railway ticket brokerage in 1890 was on the St. Louis & Iron Mountain Railway Line. Hicken also sold Huyler's candies. By 1910, he was operating a store in the Hotel Main. The Little Rock & Fort Smith Railway was a part of this line for decades, bringing freight and passengers tri-weekly from Missouri and northwest and northeast Arkansas to Fort Smith and as far south as Memphis, Tennessee; Camden, Arkansas; Hot Springs, Arkansas; and San Antonio, Texas; and out west to San Francisco. (Fort Smith Museum of History.)

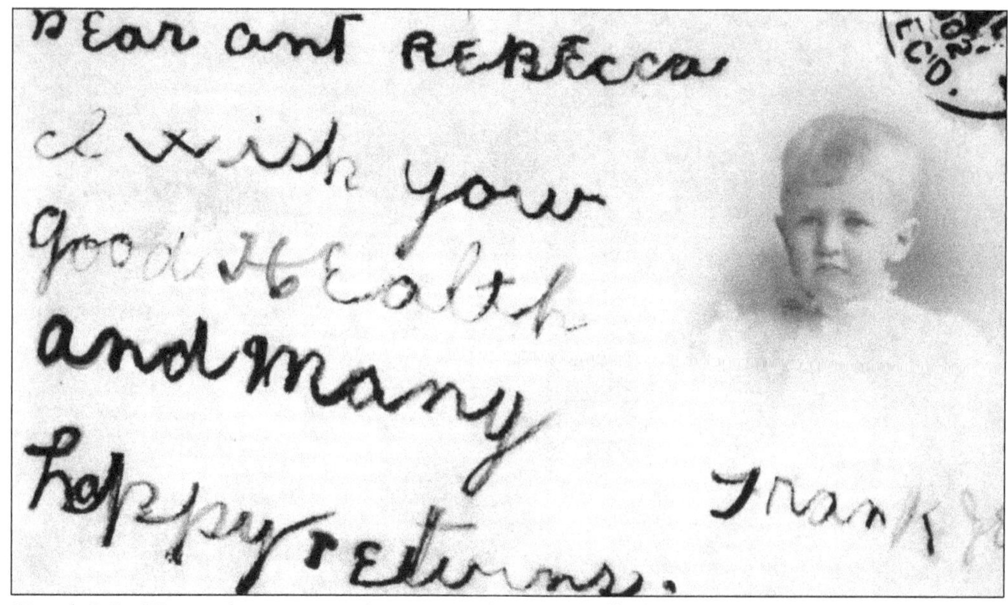
Dear aunt Rebecca
I wish you
good health
and many
happy returns.
Frank Jr.

"Frank Jr." of Pennsylvania wrote his aunt Rebecca J. (Allen) Turner, the second wife of Judge Jesse Turner Sr. of Van Buren, Arkansas, in 1902: "Dear Aunt, I wish you good health and many happy returns, Frank Jr." Rebecca Turner married Judge Turner in 1855 and lived in Van Buren. She later moved to Fort Smith and died in 1917. Lucille Price married Jesse Turner Jr., a lawyer and mayor of Van Buren (1880–1885). Jesse Jr. died in 1911. Lucille, sister of Elizabeth Price Coffey and Katherine Price Bailey, was influential in the Southwestern Studio of Musical Art of Fort Smith in the early 1900s. (Reeves, Raymond, and Bailey family collection.)

Robert Lee Casey (1868–1947) from Tennessee is seen with his second wife, Nancy Elizabeth (Byford) Casey (1885–1969), in the early 1900s. Lottie Byford Casey, Robert's first wife, was sent to Little Rock from Fort Smith on a river barge, "because they were river people and she said the wagon was too rough," when she sought cancer treatment. Robert married her sister, Nancy, after Lottie's death. The Caseys are buried in Rose Lawn Park Cemetery in Fort Smith. (R.D. Casey family collection.)

Phillip Gustave "Gus" Boehmer (1869–1951), who was born in Missouri, and John G. Limberg built the first automobile in Fort Smith in 1898. Limberg, of German descent, was born in Fort Smith and operated Limberg Brothers woodworking. He was a member of the Grand Opera House orchestra and played clarinet with John Philip Sousa's band at the 1904 World's Fair in St. Louis. The Fort Smith Shoe factory is at left. Not pictured is Gus Boehmer Jr., who would serve as a wagoner in the US Army during World War I. He died in 1962 at age 62 and is buried in Fort Smith National Cemetery. (Fort Smith Museum of History.)

Boehmer Motor Shop is pictured in 1904. Cars produced in this Fort Smith shop would run up to 20 miles per hour and ushered in the automobile business to the area. The trolley lines and wagons throughout the city would now have competition. (Bradford Randall collection.)

The increase in demand for oil from new car owners, manufacturers, farmers, and other industrial people encouraged drilling in Arkansas and Oklahoma. This is a 1910–1911 photograph near Fort Smith. Many residents put their faith in this black gold, and roughnecks and riggers of all creeds and colors began flooding the area for opportunity. The emergence of widespread drilling operations caused Native Americans more conflicts with others who wanted their land again. Some tribes, however, were drilling and mining on their lands already, such as the Chickasaw in Murry County, Oklahoma. (Fort Smith Museum of History.)

The fifth oldest Ford dealership in America was opened in Fort Smith by Paul Sheridan in October 1908. Sheridan would form a partnership with Clyde Randall. The Randalls continue to sell Fords in Fort Smith. This building was in downtown Fort Smith and was connected to a horse corral. The first Fords sold here ranged from $500 to $800. By 1916, prices had dropped to $350. (Bradford Randall collection.)

This is the interior of Sheridan Ford around 1908. Henry Ford's Model T took the country by storm beginning in October 1908 and continuing through 1927, when the 15 millionth Model T was completed. Thousands of these cars are still on the road today. The versatile Model T was good for paved or dirt roads, and many of the cars were converted through accessories for farm work. (Bradford Randall collection.)

This postcard of Garrison Avenue shows a mixture of technologies around 1910, as horse and buggy are in direct competition with the electric trolley lines. The trolleys were gone by the 1930s, and the automobile would replace horses almost entirely, but as the Great Depression and 1940s war rationing came along, many returned to their horses rather than have the hassle and costs of gasoline, oil, and car maintenance. (Arthur Berry collection.)

Written on this card is: "To my good friend Mr. John B. Williams. With sincere best wishes—Emmett Dalton. May 4th, 1931." Emmett Dalton, the only surviving member of the gang that tried to rob two Coffeyville, Kansas, banks simultaneously in broad daylight, was also once a posse raid member for the Fort Smith federal court in the 1890s. He signed this postcard for local sheriff John B. Williams. (Fort Smith National Historic Site.)

Edmund Beauregard Baker (at far left in this 1910 family photograph) served with the Fort Smith Police Department in the early 1900s and also was a drugstore representative in Branch, Franklin County, Arkansas, and in Fort Smith between 1902 and 1910, with an account at First National Bank of Fort Smith. Baker was born in 1864 in Texas and died in 1934. Pictured are, from left to right (first row) James Edmund Baker and Bill John Baker; (second row) Edmund B. Baker, Joe Y. Baker, and Louvina (Yarbrough) Baker; (third row) Daisy (Baker) Shumate (Edmund Baker's daughter by first marriage to Lily Irene Martin in 1885) and Josie Yarbrough (Lou Baker's Stepmother). Edmund and Louvenia were married in 1898. (Linoel Baker collection.)

Capt. Ed. Baker (second row, fourth from left) is seen around 1911 with the Fort Smith Police. Mayor Fagan Bourland, who began his long career as mayor in 1907, is in the first row, second from the left. Other men pictured are, from left to right, (first row) Bill Sherman, Bourland, Bill McCauley, Chief Bryant Barry, Ed Pennywell, Mike Gordon, and Mr. Fricke; (second row) Charlie Hennesy, Bill Fentress, Jim Dobbins, Baker, Omer Shaw, and Clint Hines; (third row) Tom Cantrell, T.F.B. Green, Jim Kincannon, Luther Lester, Phillip Ross, and Jim Dickey. (Linoel Baker collection.)

William Worth Bailey, born at North Second Street on March 15, 1877, was known as "the Marvelous Blind Violinist." His father, W.W. Bailey Sr., a Missouri cavalry physician who married Dr. John H.T. Main's daughter Lelia in 1868, organized St. John's/Belle Point Hospital in the 1880s. His grandfather Joseph Bailey was Fort Smith post surgeon in the mid-1800s. W.W. Bailey Jr. was advertised in 1902 as the "Blind Phenomenon" and a "New Musical Sensation." This c. 1902 photograph shows Bailey (at left) on tour in Europe. His siblings included Belle Gant of Los Angeles, Kate Bailey Parker of Fort Smith, and brother J. Mayne Bailey, who also managed his business. (Reeves, Raymond, and Bailey family collection.)

The flood of 1913 caused much damage in Fort Smith, but businesses remained open through adversity. These gentlemen provided passage to a woman at Ellison's 5¢, 10¢, and 25¢ store on Garrison Avenue. The well-dressed men are soaked to the knees. Flooding occurred frequently throughout the 20th century in Fort Smith before the Arkansas River Navigational System's series of locks and dams sought to help control the river in the 1970s. (Fort Smith Museum of History.)

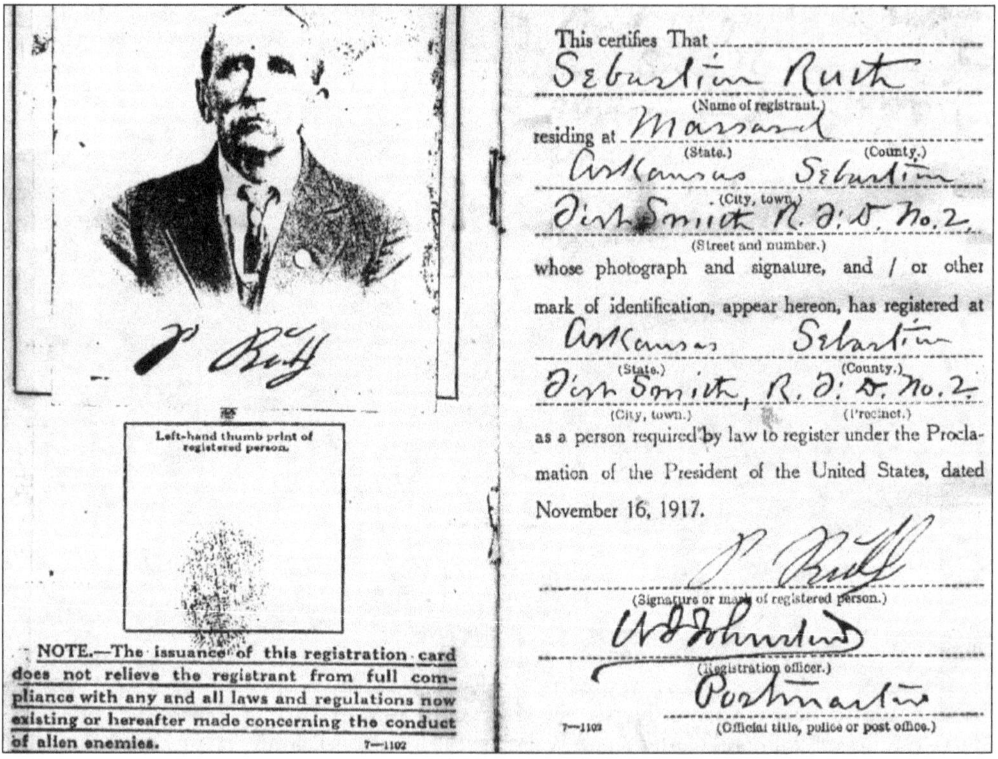

P. Ruth

Left-hand thumb print of registered person.

NOTE.—The issuance of this registration card does not relieve the registrant from full compliance with any and all laws and regulations now existing or hereafter made concerning the conduct of alien enemies. 7—1102

This certifies That Sebastian Ruth
(Name of registrant.)
residing at Massard
(State.) (County.)
Arkansas Sebastian
(City, town.)
Fort Smith R. D. No. 2
(Street and number.)
whose photograph and signature, and / or other mark of identification, appear hereon, has registered at
Arkansas Sebastian
(State.) (County.)
Fort Smith, R. D. No. 2
(City, town.) (Precinct.)
as a person required by law to register under the Proclamation of the President of the United States, dated November 16, 1917.

P. Ruth
(Signature or mark of registered person.)
W. A. Johnston
(Registration officer.)
Postmaster
7—1103 (Official title, police or post office.)

Sebastian Thomas Ruth's 1917 registration card proves his citizenship near Massard, Arkansas, during World War I. Pres. Woodrow Wilson's April and November 1917 war proclamation and promotion of removing all illegal aliens or those loyal to Germany focused on "males of the age of fourteen years and upwards, who shall be within the United States, and not actually naturalized." These men were "liable to be apprehended, restrained, secured, and removed, as alien enemies." (Rick Ruth collection.)

Two

Growing Pains, the Great Depression, and Emergence

This fire-escape view of the Weldon, Williams, and Lick property, built in 1898, provides a sample of advertisements from that time. Wharton Carnall's Real Estate is promoted on the building at right, and the first fruit-flavored chewing gum, Kiss-Me Gum, invented by Jonathan P. Primley, is shown with Budweiser beer on the fence at left. The gum advertised that it was "Far Better than a Kiss" as well as "The Best Gum in the World." Weldon, Williams, and Lick printed posters, tickets, and many graphics for companies nationwide. The company continues to this day in Fort Smith. (Fort Smith Chamber of Commerce.)

This photograph from around 1904 shows a picnic of Weldon, Williams, and Lick employees enjoying a typical Arkansas summer ritual—eating watermelon. The fertile river bottoms around Fort Smith continue to offer excellent watermelon yields. Future president Bill Clinton once claimed to his college classmates that the best watermelons were from Arkansas. (Fort Smith Museum of History.)

The first firehouse in Fort Smith was built at Walnut (now A) and Sixth Streets. This photograph from 1907 shows the chief's car and the pumpers. Visitors to the Fort Smith Museum of History can see one of these old machines that were used to fight fires in Fort Smith. (Fort Smith Museum of History.)

Pictured here are members of the Sixth Street firehouse. From left to right are (first row) Bob Coon, unidentified, Chief Morris Brun, two unidentified, and Pink Dean; (second row) all unidentified; (third row) John Roberts, five unidentified, and Allen Etter; (fourth row) unidentified, John Dixon, unidentified, Cecil Norfleet, and four unidentified. The firemen were identified by Marie Eslinger, niece of fireman Joe Cantrell. (Myrna Wells collection.)

In the days before moving vans, residents called upon the services of John David Mincher (1850–1937) and his wagon. Mincher, who made his living as a mover, was the great-grandfather of Myrna Wells. He is buried in Oak Cemetery. (Myrna Wells collection.)

Joseph Cantrell was a Fort Smith fireman in the early 1900s. He married Ester Pearl Mincher in 1908. Joseph died at 28 and is buried in Oak Cemetery. The Woodmen of the World erected his monument. Joseph and Ester lived with her parents in the 300 or 400 block of South Twelfth Street. Most men in the area fought fires as volunteers; those few who were paid firemen earned between $10 and $25 a month. (Myrna Wells collection.)

This miller wagon is from the early 1900s. The Big Four Milling Company advertised bringing flour, grain, and hay from its Fourth Street location in Fort Smith. Other prominent companies in the area included the Fort Smith Grain Company, "flour and feed handlers," organized in 1917; Durrett Flour and Grain, which increased its capital to $50,000 in 1917; and the Interstate Grain Company, which was chartered that year with $30,000 capital by J.F. Fair, C. Wenderoth, William C. Lovely, H.C. Osbourne, and Eugene Davidson. (Myrna Wells collection.)

Ida Adeline Ainsworth Bowles (at left) was born in the Choctaw Nation to Maggie (Collins) and John Garrett Ainsworth, near present-day Spiro, Oklahoma, in 1881. She married Elijah "Lydge" Bishop at Fort Smith in 1900. Her father shot Bishop after an argument near Skullyville, Indian Territory, in 1906. Ainsworth was said to have killed over 10 men but never saw a courtroom. Bishop was buried at Paw Paw, in Sequoyah County. Ida remarried between 1906 and 1910 to Nicholas Houston "Charles/Charlie" Bowles. Maggie (Bowles) Turnipseed was one of the daughters of this second marriage. (Nick Janes and Maggie Janes Jones collection.)

This c. 1913 view of Garrison Avenue, looking toward Fifth Street, shows the First National Bank of Fort Smith on the left (built in 1911) next to the Hotel Main and the Merchants National Bank at right, which was completed in 1912. Klein and Fink jewelers are at far right, and the Nathan Clothing Company is across the street at left. (Fort Smith Museum of History.)

This 1920s photograph shows Lincoln High School and Manual Training Center in north Fort Smith. Built in 1892, this originally redbrick school was for African Americans until desegregation closed the school and directed students to Northside High School in Fort Smith. The last senior class at Lincoln High was in 1966. (Fort Smith Museum of History.)

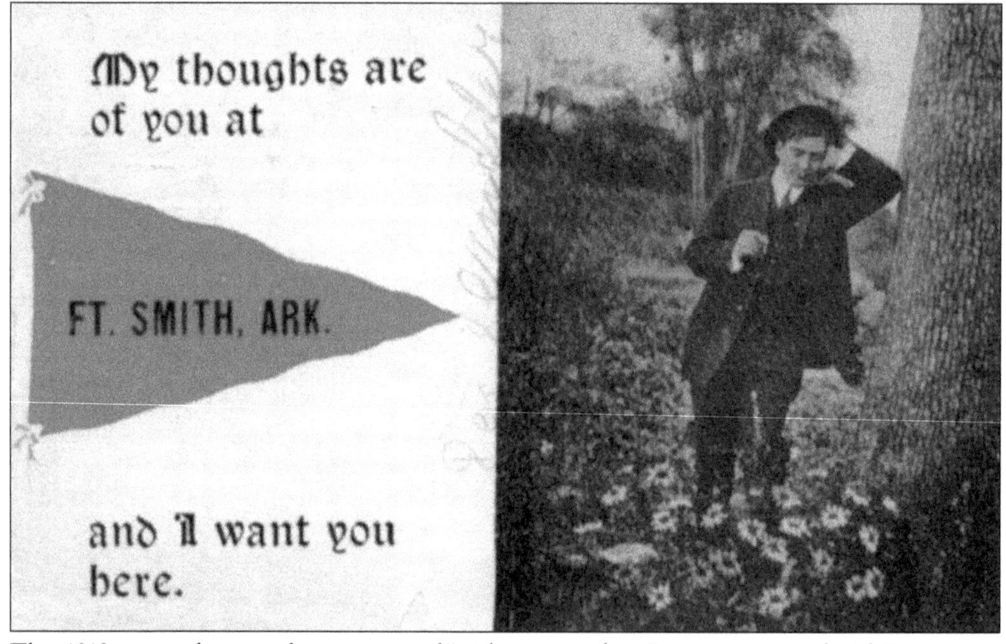

This 1913 postcard is one of many types of "wish you were here" sentiments used with "your town name inserted here" for business travelers and tourists. Cards such as this one were sold in many stores on Garrison Avenue in Fort Smith until World War I. (Fort Smith Museum of History.)

Thomas V. Gray, manager of the auto division at Atkinson-Williams Hardware in Fort Smith during the 1920s, stands in front of the Atkinson-Williams Building, which now houses the Fort Smith Museum of History. (Fort Smith Museum of History.)

A road-building crew packs down gravel during the 1920s to prepare for the influx of new automobiles near what is now Free-Ferry Road and Rogers Avenue. Most of the workers are African American, and the road paver is powered by what appears to be a 1911-era Case steam engine. (Fort Smith Museum of History.)

This view across Garrison Avenue from the Goldman Hotel looks southeast toward an area of what is now Rogers Avenue toward North Fourteenth, A, and B Streets. Bancorp South Bank and Immaculate Conception School are now in these areas, but a variation of the gas station at the corner exists, and the house at top center on the southwest corner of B and Fourteenth Streets still stands today. (Fort Smith Museum of History.)

This photograph shows an early printing shop on Garrison Avenue using electric moving presses. The machines are similar to Chandler and Price letterpresses made in 1923. Letterpress printing embosses the images and lettering to the page in a more tactile way that has become popular again in recent years for invitations, book binding, and special poster making and print making nationwide. The University of Arkansas at Fort Smith's Underground Ink letterpress shop offers classes in these older technologies that have returned to graphic art studies and wide commercial usage. (Fort Smith Museum of History.)

Mary Breckinridge (left) and her son Clifford Breckinridge "Breckie" Thompson met with Lucille P. Turner at the Crescent Hotel in Eureka Springs, Arkansas, prior to 1918. Mary moved here with second husband Richard R. Thompson from Fort Smith in 1908. Thompson was Crescent College and Conservatory president until 1924. Mary taught French and hygiene. A daughter, Mary "Polly," died at six hours old in 1916, and Breckie died of appendicitis in 1918 at the Crescent. Mary divorced her cheating husband in 1920, worked to rebuild war-torn France, and trained as a midwife in England. She organized the Frontier Nursing Service at Wendover, Kentucky, in 1925 and supported rights for women and children until her death in 1965. (Reeves, Raymond, and Bailey family collection.)

William Armistead Falconer (Sebastian County judge from 1902 to 1908 and an Arkansas state railroad commissioner) was born in 1868 at Charleston, Arkansas, to John T. and Fannie F. Falconer, dry goods merchants of Fort Smith. Educated at the University of Arkansas and the University of Virginia, Falconer attended St. John's Episcopal Church with W.W. Bailey, Elizabeth P. Coffey, and others. Falconer died in 1922 and was buried in Forest Park Cemetery in Fort Smith. (Reeves, Raymond, and Bailey family collection.)

The home of Urban G. and Theresa Sharum and their two barns were located near Massard, Arkansas. The far right barn is south of Phoenix Avenue in Fort Smith. Everything in this image is now Eighty-seventh Street and Rogers Avenue. Confederates attacked foraging Federal troops in July 1864 south of this location near Millennium Street. The Battle of Massard Prairie was a sneak attack as Confederates sought to enter Fort Smith. Texas and Choctaw Confederates led by Brig. Gen. R.M. Gano attacked 200 of the Kansas 6th Cavalry, killing 10, wounding 17, and capturing 117. This Confederate victory secured weapons and supplies for the needy men. Rebels lost 10 men over the two-mile battle, including Choctaw Tiok-homma, also known as "Red Pine," who was noted for bravery. The large trenches dug for the dead have never been found. (Rick Ruth family collection.)

Cornelius "Neely" Lafayette Sharum and Josephine (née Bury) Sharum (left) are standing with Urban and Theresa (née Bury) Sharum in Massard, Arkansas. Cornelius and Josie operated a grocery at what is now Massard Road and Rogers Avenue while Urban and Theresa farmed and owned the U.G. and L.A. Sharum General Store, located northwest of Massard Bridge. (Evangeline Werner collection.)

This Cornelius Sharum store sack advertises "All-Star Brand Shoes from Roberts, Johnson, and Rand Shoe Co. of St. Louis" found in the C.L. Sharum & Brothers General Merchandise, near Fort Smith. This sack is the property of Steve Sharum of Fort Smith, grandson of Cornelius Sharum. (Steve Sharum collection.)

Cornelius "Neely" Lafayette Sharum and Urban Gustave Sharum's store was in Massard, Arkansas, across Highway 22 from the Methodist Church. C.L. (the youngest of 10 children) was 15 years younger than his brother, Urban, the fourth child. Neely Sharum died in 1946, and U.G. Sharum died in 1949. Josephine and Theresa Bury were sisters who married the two Sharum brothers. The Ruth family later owned the store. (Evangeline Werner collection.)

These painters are, from left to right, L.J. Belew and the famous Fort Smith area mover John D. Mincher. Catherine "Kate" Mincher (1887–1970) married Charles Clark Akers (1883–1936) and later L.J. Belew of Spiro, Oklahoma. A Mrs. Moore is standing in the doorway of her café on Towson Avenue in Fort Smith. (Myrna Wells collection.)

The reverse of this photograph reads, "Taken Sunday Night May 15, 1921 Master's Electric Company Show window. Girl in window, supposed to be hypnotized, slept from 4 p.m., Sunday, May 15 until 9 p.m., May 16, 1921. 809 and 811 Garrison Avenue Fort Smith Arkansas." (Fort Smith Museum of History.)

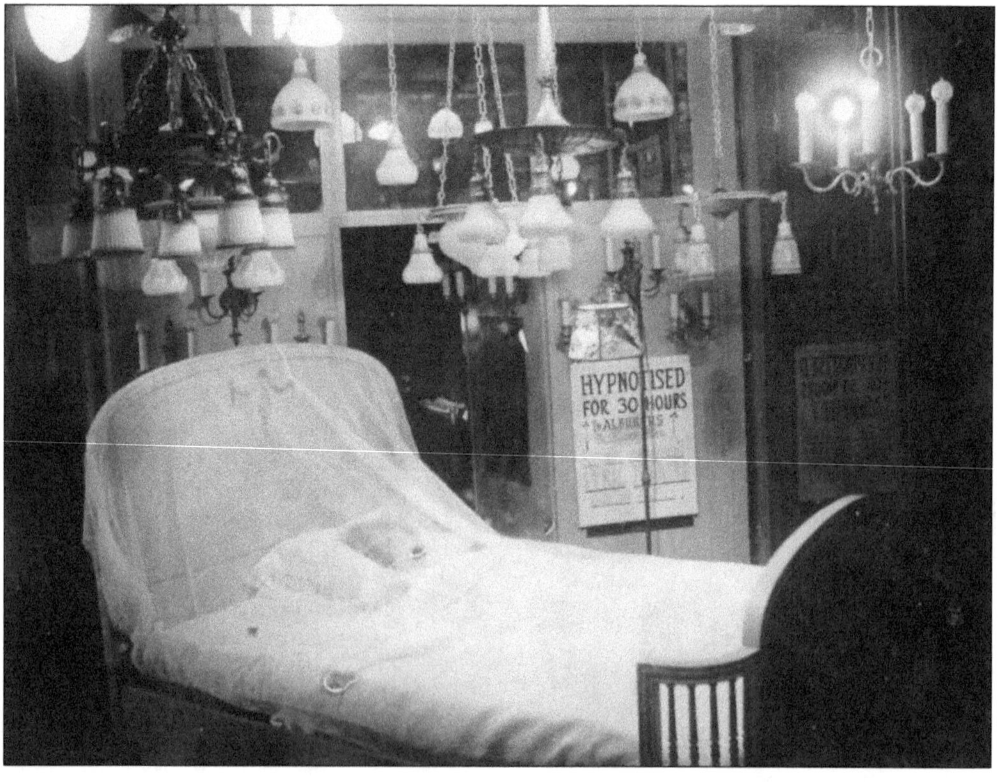

Many then-new innovations, like natural gas lines and the gas station, are visible in this 1920s river valley photograph, and an economic boost accompanied these services. People in the area went to Sheridan/Randall Ford to purchase cars. The Oklahoma Gas and Electric Company started on wells in Arkansas and Oklahoma in the early 20th century, which still influence the local economy and way of life today. (Fort Smith Museum of History.)

The Church of St. Boniface and parsonage at North Nineteenth Street in Fort Smith are shown in the 1920s. The white church here is commonly referred to as the first church, but Arthur Berry notes it was the third, as a log church built in 1847 served as the first and an 1867 wood frame church was the second, none of which exist. The structure in this photograph was built by German immigrants in 1887 and was torn down to make way for a new school and church. (Fort Smith Museum of History.)

Pictured in the 1920s, the St. Boniface School was built in 1913. From the 1880s to today, some families have belonged to the church for many generations. The church and school are an integral part of the history and culture of Fort Smith. (Fort Smith Museum of History.)

The Church of St. Boniface at North B Street was named after the patron saint of Germany. Arthur "Artie" Berry completed a history of the stained-glass windows, which were brought from Munich and installed in 1939. This structure was remodeled in 2002. This church has 42 relics, more than any other Catholic church in the area, according to Rev. Jon McDougal, pastor since 2004. (Arthur Berry collection.)

Paul Slack's Mayos Clothes store was at 618 Garrison Avenue. This exterior image is from the 1930s. Kate Akers (center) was the store's seamstress. The man on the right appears to be Paul Slack. The man on the left is unidentified. (Myrna Wells collection.)

The interior of Paul Slack's Mayos Clothing store shows a variety of fashions from the era. Kate Akers was the seamstress at the center of the three ladies; the other two women are unidentified. The man at right is Paul Slack, the owner of the store. (Myrna Wells collection.)

Trolley No. 65 on Little Rock Road is ready to roll with conductor Charles Akers (left) around 1912. Parts of Little Rock Road are now considered Rogers Avenue in Fort Smith. This car is parked by Oak Cemetery on what is now Old Greenwood Road. Oak Cemetery is one of the oldest in the city. Charles Clark Akers (1883–1936), born to Jonathan and Mary Catherine Akers, married Catherine "Kate" Mincher. (Myrna Wells collection.)

A parade near Sixth Street during World War I sought to raise funds and promote the "Second War Fund." The Great War of 1914–1919 was to be the war to end all wars; however, the devastation it caused encouraged many young people to become members of "the Lost Generation." The Fort Smith Wagon Company had 206 subscribers for the Second War Fund. (Pebley Center, Boreham Library, University of Arkansas at Fort Smith.)

During World War I, many cities in America celebrated troops leaving and coming home, and good news in general. Although the war began in Europe in 1914, the United States remained neutral until German U-boats increased their attacks on American ships. The sinking of the *Lusitania* and other actions forced the United States into the war. This photograph of Garrison Avenue is assumed to be during a 1917 war bond drive. (Fort Smith Museum of History.)

Pictured are the past mayors of Fort Smith, up to 1917, with the newly adopted municipal flag of Fort Smith on the right and the banner of the Lions Club, one of the oldest civic organizations in the area. Among those pictured are W.J. Johnston (1909–1911); Fagan Bourland (1907–1908, 1911–1913, 1921–1923, and 1929–1933), second from left; Henry C. Read (1913–1917), who proclaimed the new flag in 1916; John H. Wright (1917); and Arch Monroe (1917–1921). (Fort Smith Museum of History.)

The versatile cars of the 1920s were probably not designed as boats, but the 1927 flood in Fort Smith tested the limits of these automobiles' endurance. As usual, Fort Smith citizens were resilient and pushed through adversity. This scene is looking west on Rogers Avenue toward Fifth Street. (Fort Smith Museum of History.)

Boy Scouts are seen in the 1917 American Legion Round-up on Garrison Avenue, looking toward Texas Corner at left and Immaculate Conception Church. During World War I, scouts served as radio defense, coastal patrols, and draft watchers. The Boy Scouts of America nationwide sold $352 million in war bonds and $101 million in War Saving Stamps, collected fruit pits for charcoal in gas masks, and counted walnut trees for propellers and gunstocks. Scouting today helps local food banks and various community and conservation service projects to promote service and honor to others, to God, and to the United States. (Fort Smith Museum of History.)

Catherine "Kate" Mincher Akers Belew is promoting the war effort around 1917. Fort Smith, like many towns in America, decorated homes and businesses for solidarity. Over 2,000 people attended a dedication for a 1930 statue honoring the World War I soldiers. The monument to the doughboys was placed in Tilles Park and later moved to the American Legion post on Midland Avenue. (Myrna Wells collection.)

This parade is typical of many during the mid-20th century. Garrison Avenue continues to offer large Christmas, St. Patrick's Day, and rodeo parades. After the Armistice of 1919, the Roaring Twenties and the Jazz Age were born. The Lost Generation scattered throughout the United States and the world looking for meaning, but most people kept to the tasks they had before the conflict. An era of expansion, bootlegging, crime, stock inflation, and technological and cultural innovation hit the nation. (Fort Smith Museum of History.)

The offices of Oklahoma Gas and Electric are at left, and a sliver of the Goldman Hotel is at right in this 1930s image. The photograph was taken from the steps of Immaculate Conception Church. Gone are the trolley lines that stretched down the middle of Garrison Avenue, as well as the horses and wagons, which faded into rural use. (Fort Smith Museum of History.)

Here is a view of the Avenue from the opposite direction, looking east from near Fifth Street. The Ward Hotel, built in 1929 with 165 rooms, remains the tallest building at 140 feet on Garrison Avenue. By the 1950s, the Ward increased to 200 rooms. The hotel closed in the 1970s and serves now as office space and storage for many local businesses. (Fort Smith Museum of History.)

The buildings at left are across from the courthouses near Sixth Street in Fort Smith. The *Southwest American* and *Times-Record* newspapers, as well as Quality Auto, were housed here in the 1920s. (Fort Smith Museum of History.)

This perspective is from South Sixth Street in Fort Smith looking north toward Garrison Avenue before World War I. The First National Bank of Fort Smith is clearly visible in the center of the photograph, and beyond that is the Southern Hotel. (Fort Smith Museum of History.)

The Princess Theater is at right in this 1917 image. A musical comedy is advertised for this space managed by John Mayne (Main) Bailey, brother of William Worth Bailey, the blind violin virtuoso. To the far right is the ornate Boston Store, which occupied this location from the 1890s until 1971, when it moved to Central Mall on Rogers Avenue and later closed in 1986. (Fort Smith Museum of History.)

The new Fort Smith High School at Twenty-third and B Streets was needed as the city grew to over 30,000 residents. Northside High School was established here in 1961. Alumni include Sen. John Boozman and athletes Ron Brewer and Matt Jones. Classes for Fort Smith Junior College were taught here also from the 1920s until 1950, when Westark Junior College moved to Grand and Waldron Avenues. Westark became the University of Arkansas at Fort Smith in 2001. The school is pictured here in 1928. (Fort Smith Museum of History.)

This pre-1937 photograph of Garrison Avenue and Towson Avenue (Texas Road and Texas Corner), looking west, shows many buildings that have since been destroyed by fire, neglect, or weather. The Friedman-Mincer Building (far left), built in 1912, is currently in shambles. It once housed an Otasco (Oklahoma Tire and Supply Company) store for decades. The Kansas City Southern Union Station, constructed in 1913, can be seen at middle left. This structure was torn down in the 1960s, and a Holiday Inn stands there today. (Fort Smith Museum of History.)

This February 8, 1929, image shows Union Station at the 700 block of Rogers Avenue—with snow on the ground. Leota C. Pettigrew is assumed to be one of the women in the photograph. Pettigrew was a longtime Sebastian County employee until 1956. (Fort Smith Museum of History.)

St. John's Episcopal Church is pictured in the 1940s. The church was built in 1900 at 215 North Sixth Street; the tower was added in 1912. The church originated in 1838 with the baptism of Elias Rector's children. George Birnie provided land in the 1860s for a new building at Knox (now Sixth) Street and Sycamore (now C) Street. The church and its members are affiliated with the Next Step, a local organization that helps homeless people receive food, shelter, and supplies and helps them return to work; the church also offers a Good Samaritan Clinic and helps the needy in the area. (Fort Smith Museum of History.)

The Star Grocery Store opened in 1909 at 717 Garrison Avenue. The Star was the first self-serve modern grocery in Fort Smith. (Fort Smith Museum of History.)

The Lutheran church, school, and parsonage are pictured between 1922 and 1940 at North Twelfth and D Streets. This church began in 1869 facing North D Street between Eleventh and Twelfth Streets, and the main church building in this photograph was completed in 1904. Electric lights and gas emergency lights were added in 1911, according to church history. John Schaap and S.A. Williams were parishioners in the 1800s. (Fort Smith Museum of History.)

First Presbyterian Church, pictured in 1925, was organized in 1846. The church was completed in 1900, with a cornerstone of 1898. A school was added in 1920, and it was reconstructed in 1962 and continues to serve many young children. (Fort Smith Museum of History.)

Mallalieu Methodist Church was formed in the 1800s as an African American Methodist Church. The structure at 800 North Ninth Street was built in 1921 and was used until the 1980s. Plans in 2000 called for a multicultural center, but these were scrapped by the city due to renovation costs and asbestos removal. The city demolished the building, leaving a facade in place. Pleas from Dr. Paul Beran, chancellor of the University of Arkansas at Fort Smith, and city officials suggested a joint venture to utilize the area for a center and library annex to save at-risk students and increase education in the northern neighborhoods of Fort Smith. The project is currently on hold. (Fort Smith Museum of History.)

Kansas City Southern (KCS) Railroad engine No. 400 is pictured here. Although a little older, it is one that may have run through Fort Smith's Union Station after 1913. The Texarkana & Fort Smith Railway, a subsidiary of KCS, was organized in 1885. Eventually, lines ran from Kansas City through Fort Smith and Mena, Arkansas, to the Gulf of Mexico. These lines are still used today for freight through Missouri to Texas. (Fort Smith Museum of History.)

The train yard and platforms of Kansas City Southern and Frisco Lines Union Station are viewed over the Nathan Clothing store from Garrison Avenue southward. The Alamo Boardinghouse is at far left. This area south of the station continues to be the site of many industries and milling operations vital to Fort Smith, including Yaffe Iron, Glover Machine Works, OK Foods, Davis Iron and Metal, Clayton Consulting and Welding, Dyke Lumber Company, and Hiland Dairy. (Pebley Center, Boreham Library, University of Arkansas at Fort Smith.)

A busy day on Garrison Avenue reveals Wirsing's Sporting Goods and Repair Store, among wholesale grocers and the Eagle Clothing Store. Will Wirsing claimed to have acquired Cherokee Bill's .38–56 1886 Winchester from a federal jailer in 1896 after Bill's execution. He was featured in the *Sporting Goods Dealer* magazine and *American Rifleman* in 1937. He died in 1938, and Chris Wirsing later sold the gun in 1971 to Preston Rose, who sold it to Bruce Bartlett in 1998. (Fort Smith Museum of History.)

Merchants National Bank is pictured as it appeared in the 1920s. This building now houses the Fort Smith city offices. Merchants National was established in 1882 and continues at 723 Garrison Avenue. William Fadjo Cravens Jr. (1929–2012) served as vice president of this bank for 31 years and was instrumental in preserving Fort Smith history. He obtained a degree in history from the University of Arkansas at Fayetteville. William Fadjo Cravens Jr. was the son of William F. Cravens Sr. and grandson to William Ben Cravens, who both served in the US House of Representatives (Fort Smith Museum of History.)

Here is the interior of Atkinson-Williams machine shop. Many of the signs from this era in this building are now housed in the Fort Smith Museum of History. The business specialized in "shelf and heavy hardware, tinware, sporting goods, and auto accessories," according to a 1926 issue of the *Guardian* newspaper. (Fort Smith Museum of History.)

The Boston Store is photographed at night on Garrison Avenue in the 1940s. "Any Book In This Window" cost 50¢, according to one sign. The store handled various types of clothing for men and women and offered a tearoom; the store was one of the central department stores of the city for decades. Ida Lue (Turnipseed) Janes worked here in the 1950s and had fond memories of the store and what it meant to the people of Fort Smith. The Fort Smith Museum of History offers frequent fashion shows and exhibits about the store. (Fort Smith Museum of History.)

Maggie Bowles, daughter of Ida Adeline Bowles and Charlie Bowles, married William Ellsworth "Bill" Turnipseed, son of John Bartlett and Lurena (Bishop) Turnipseed, in the 1920s. They had four children, Ida Lue, John W., Lena Mae Catherine, and Billie J. Maggie's husband, Bill, was a miner near Midland and Greenwood, Arkansas, as well as one of the first and longest-serving drivers for Jones Truck Lines in Fort Smith. He was also a semiprofessional ballplayer in Fort Smith. He died in 1971. Maggie lived much of her life in Arkoma, Oklahoma, and died in 1988. (Nick Janes and Maggie Janes Jones collection.)

Pictured in 1925, Belle Grove School, erected in 1886 at 600 North Sixth Street, is the largest building in the Belle Grove historic district and was the first public school in Fort Smith. In 1984, it became Belle Grove Schoolhouse Apartments. To the south of this school is the home of William Henry Harrison Clayton, who lived there from 1882 to 1897. Clayton was a federal prosecuting attorney in Parker's court and later served as a federal judge in Oklahoma. He is buried in the Fort Smith National Cemetery. He and his wife, Florence Barnes, raised seven children, with four living to 1920, the time of William Clayton's death. (Fort Smith Museum of History.)

"Mouth of the Poteau From Coke Hill, April 15, 1927 Moffett in distance," was written on this image looking toward Moffett, Oklahoma, across the Arkansas River at flood stage. The vantage point is Belle Point (site of the original Fort Smith) and Coke Hill, which was a type of Hooverville of scrap houses and make-do living until the 1950s, when officials forced residents out to establish the Fort Smith National Historic Site in 1961. At that time, an excavation of the 1817 Fort Smith was performed. (Fort Smith Museum of History.)

This 1940s photograph shows the Jewish synagogue at the corner of Eleventh and E Streets. According to the Fort Smith Museum of History, nearly 400 people attended this temple, built in 1892. This structure was sold to the First Lutheran Church, and the new United Hebrew Temple was constructed at Forty-seventh Street in the 1950s. Many of the early business and civic leaders of Fort Smith from the 1910s to 1940, including Iser Nakdimen, were immigrants who started this temple. The stone arch of this building serves as the West End Park entrance on Second Street today. (Fort Smith Museum of History.)

The Kress Store at 812 Garrison Avenue was under construction in 1911 in this photograph. Seymour Burrell designed it. Edward F. Sibbert completed the current facade of the building in 1939. This building remains one of the unique architectural features of downtown and the Art Deco movement of that era. The store closed in 1974. (Fort Smith Museum of History.)

This home, pictured around 1914, was built on land originally part of the William Fishback estate at Rogers Avenue and Adelaide Street in Fort Smith. Fishback was a former governor of Arkansas. This historic neighborhood offers many homes of various styles of early-20th-century American architectural movements. This home is now the offices of Fleming-Lau Realty. (Bailey family collection.)

Located at 321 North Twelfth Street and Grand Avenue in 1912, the Southwestern Studio of Musical Art provided a broad education for local residents for many years. The director and treasurer, Katherine Price Bailey, and the president and violin teacher, her husband, William Worth Bailey, created the Fort Smith Symphony with their former and then-current students in 1923. The Fort Smith Symphony is the oldest in the state of Arkansas. (Reeves, Raymond, and Bailey family collection.)

The faculty and staff of the Southwestern Studios of Musical Art are shown here. Pictured are, from left to right, (first row) Virginia Merritt Beck and Hattie May Butterfield; (second row) Anna Green Scott, Lucille Price Turner, and Anna Rose Miller; (third row) two unidentified, Elizabeth Price Coffey, unidentified, William W. Bailey, and Katherine Price Bailey. Lucille, Elizabeth, and Katherine were sisters. Lucille was married to Jesse Turner Jr. of Van Buren. Note that William and Katherine are holding hands. (Reeves, Raymond, and Bailey family collection.)

This is a Southwestern Studios of Musical Art piano class around 1925. Lucille Price Turner stands at the piano. Lucille was vice president of Southwestern and taught the musical history courses and English literature. She held an Oxford Honors of the First Class in English literature degree from Oxford University in England, and published poetry. She earned $2 per student per weekly lesson. Lucille's husband was mayor of Van Buren and a lawyer. He died in 1911. She died in 1964. (Reeves, Raymond, and Bailey family collection.)

The Fort Smith Symphony performed *Elijah*, directed by Katherine Price Bailey, at the Masonic temple at North Eleventh and B Streets around 1929. Many have spoken of the elaborate scenes portrayed on the stage and of the movies they watched in the temple. The land was purchased for $49,000 and the general contract was made on June 11, 1927, for $208,500. Furnishings and equipment brought the total to $385,000. The historic temple is now looking for a buyer, as is the Malco New Theatre on Tenth Street. Both spaces deserve preservation. (Fort Smith Museum of History.)

Choir practice is seen here with choir director Elizabeth Price Coffey (at left, front) at St. John's Episcopal Church between 1925 and 1935. Lucille Price Turner and Katherine Price Bailey are also at left. William W. Bailey is standing with his violin and bow on the altar behind the boy in the middle. (Reeves, Raymond, and Bailey family collection.)

Elizabeth Price Coffey is seen in a 1920s photograph. A distinguished pianist who often accompanied her brother-in-law William W. Bailey, the blind violin virtuoso, she was present at festivities at Subiaco in 1912 and Msgr. Patrick Horan's silver jubilee at Immaculate Conception Church. Additionally, she accompanied vocalist Irene DuBois and violinist Maurice Derdeyn at a Guild Tea at St. Anne's Convent in Fort Smith in 1921. (Reeves, Raymond, and Bailey family collection.)

Anna Green Scott was a first violin in the New Theatre Orchestra for 10 years and a founding member of the Fort Smith Symphony. She studied with John B. Kimball at Trinidad, Colorado, Carl Stevenson of New York City, and Katherine Price Bailey of Fort Smith. She taught violin lessons at Southwestern Studios of Musical Art. (Bailey family collection.)

Anna Rose Miller taught piano in Fort Smith for many years. She was a pupil of Elizabeth Price Coffey, Hattie Mae Butterfield, and Pearl Jarrard. She also studied in St. Louis, Missouri, at the Progressive Series College and was a part of the Southwestern Studios of Musical Art when this picture was taken in 1930. (Bailey family collection.)

Trained at the Southwestern Studio of Musical Art, Margaret Woodrow Beck taught at the Southwestern Studios, Sallisaw, and Cameron, Oklahoma. She was director of music for the public schools in Cameron, taught piano and theory, and directed the choir. She was also an organist at the First Church of Christian Scientists, Fort Smith. She was a sponsor of the Alpha Pi Mu National Music Society in Fort Smith and the Pi Mu Juvenal Society. She was the city chair of the National Music Week Committee of Fort Smith and Press Committee of the Musical Coterie. (Bailey family collection.)

Irene DuBois was recognized as one of Fort Smith's most accomplished vocal artists. DuBois, a mezzo-soprano, who often sang at the Christian Science church, served as a member of the Scottish Rite Choir, was director of the Fort Smith Business and Professional Women's Glee Club, and a member of the Fort Smith Choral Club. She studied at the American Conservatory in Chicago and at Southwestern in Fort Smith. She was also one of the first vocalists with the original Fort Smith Symphony and taught piano for beginners at the Southwestern Studios of Musical Art. (Bailey family collection.)

Hattie May Butterfield (shown in 1930) taught piano, organ, and music history at Southwestern in the 1930s and was much in demand as an organist in the area. She played organ at St. John's Episcopal Church and later taught music at Westark Junior College. She earned a doctorate in fine arts and is buried in Forest Park Cemetery. The University of Arkansas at Fort Smith offers a Hattie May Butterfield memorial scholarship in music. Margaret Montague taught dramatic art and expression at Southwestern and later worked with Butterfield at Westark for many years. (Bailey family collection.)

Ruth Hunt graduated from Tennessee College at Murfreesboro with a bachelor of arts in music. She studied piano with Stanley Levy and was a student at Southwestern Studios in Fort Smith. She taught piano and theory at Southwestern in 1930 and served as the pianist of Emmanuel Baptist Church in Fort Smith. (Bailey family collection.)

Here are students of the Southwestern Studios of Musical Art in the 1930s. Southwestern offered four-year college credit in cooperation with Fort Smith Junior College for a bachelor's in music, teaching certificates, literature, languages, and dramatic art and expression. William W. Bailey died in 1932 of heart disease at 54. By all accounts, he was an excellent musician and a good man. He is buried in the Turner plot at Fairview Cemetery in Van Buren, Arkansas. Bailey, a student of Ovid Musante in Europe, was the composer of "The Song of the Pines," often called his most perfect composition. His wife, Katherine, published hundreds of poems and was the director of the Fort Smith Symphony until 1946. She continued to teach and died at 102 in 1985. (Bailey family collection.)

Virginia Merritt Beck Hefner taught violin and piano at Southwestern, beginning violin lessons with Katherine Price Bailey at age eight and piano with Emma Ewing Price at age six. She won several statewide awards in the 1920s and taught music at Sallisaw, Oklahoma. She was also a vocalist with the Weckoneller Trio. (Bailey family collection.)

Ella Allen's *Kiddie Corner* was broadcast on Saturday mornings from the Goldman Hotel lobby. This 1936 photograph was taken at KFPW's top floor studio in the Goldman. Pictured from left to right are (first row, on floor) Bill Allen, Miles Friedman, Roger Joyce, and Carl Wortz; (second row, sitting) unidentified, Martha Doris Shipley, Jopan Reaty, and Jane Warner; (third row, standing) Betty Jane Ragland, Jane Cutting, Ed Dell Wortz, and Annis Lick. (Fort Smith Museum of History.)

Little Studio of Dramatics of KFPW studios is pictured in the 1930s at the Goldman Hotel. KFPW began in 1930 at the top floor of the Goldman. The station continues at Pharis Broadcasting Studios on Greenwood Road in Fort Smith The Goldman, on North Thirteenth Street, closed in 1974 and was torn down in 1995. (University of Arkansas Little Rock Special Collections/ Fort Smith Museum of History.)

Jimmie Grace and his Ozarkans played through the 1930s, including a premiere for *Our Leading Citizen* in Fort Smith and Van Buren. The film starred Van Buren native Bob Burns, as well as actress Susan Hayward. In addition to Burns and Hayward, singer Eddie Arnold was at the premiere to support the film in 1939. The Ozarkans were broadcast to the nation on WBBM Chicago that day. Harold Phelps, D.J. Lane, Allen Hall, Hunter Wright, "Benny" Gordan, Foster Merk, "Putt" Robinson, Lowell Hoffman, Jimmy Pierce, Arthur Rosenbaum, Ted Hoffman, Kathryn Moody, Mary Jane Reynolds, Monte Jean Wisdom, Ola Mae Canady, Carl Adams, Denny Crofton, Bob Gilchrist, Elizabeth Rothenberger, Pete Hammock, and Gene Apple played with the Ozarkans through the decade. (Fort Smith Museum of History.)

Here, the Southerners played at the Masonic temple in 1929. From left to right are Lucien Sabin, E.F. "Putt" Robinson, Bedford "Benny" Gordon, Morgan Gallagher, Hunter Wright, Foster Merk, Arlie Holman, Miles Hershey, Louise Clark, and Gene Reynolds. Other members included Fred Williams, Dorothy Gibson, Lawrence Richardson, and Paul Comstock. KFPW broadcast the Southerners, the Ozarkans, the Charles McGill Quartet, Fred O'Baugh, Billy Beard, Joe Leming Jr., the Ridge Runners, Charles Harrison, Wilson Castleberry, Laura Schmuck, Bob McDowell, Ralph B. Jones, and Leo Maestri on October 4, 1930, along with game three of the World Series. Philadelphia beat St. Louis in four games. (Fort Smith Museum of History/Fort Smith Historical Society.)

Clint Fisher and his Musical Buddies, from left to right, Ray Gann, Fisher, Lyman Fisher, Amos Hedrick, and Buddy Covert played on stage, at military bases, and for radio shows with announcer Pat Porta. Members included William Coffman Jr., Glenn Mann, J.D. Cox, Marvin Shaw, Peewee Clark, Marion Mondier, Dubert Dobson, Peewee Calhoun, Bobby Lee, Marvin McCullough, Frankie Kirby, Bill Hayes, Walter Schleif, Bob Revell, Roy Hunnicutt, booking agent Ralph Gann, Gene Crownover, Wally McDougal, Kenneth Holliway, C.B. White, Dempsey Wright, and Henry "Hank" Eshelman. (Fort Smith Museum of History/Fort Smith Historical Society.)

Oral Stallings was a route sales supervisor for Colonial Baking Company in this 1935 photograph. Wortz Baking Company would later use this building. Stallings served in Patton's army during World War II and was a 32nd-degree Mason. He was the first Fort Smith Gerber employee and served as a manager until 1974. He lived to be 97 and is buried in Fort Smith National Cemetery. (Sherrell Buchanan collection.)

Immaculate Conception School was built at B and South Fourteenth Streets in 1930. Many of the current teachers, administration, and staff are former students of this Catholic school. It has a long tradition of academic excellence and service to the community. Additionally, Immaculate Conception School students field excellent Quiz Bowl, Battle of the Books, and athletic teams annually. Students, teachers, and volunteers also maintain an outdoor habitat for classroom projects and put on the popular annual spring festival and spaghetti dinner downtown. (Immaculate Conception School Archives.)

The Athletic Tea Company out of 721 Main Street in Kansas City, Missouri, sold its product in many stores on Garrison Avenue for years. Valentine Vogel, John C.H. Vogel, and Emil C. Stocker started the company in March 1915. The West End Drugstore and Friend Photo Supply Company (with Max W. Friend as manager) in this photograph was at 317 Garrison Avenue. (Fort Smith Museum of History.)

Here is the 1930 graduating class of Fort Smith Junior College, which later became Westark Junior College and today's University of Arkansas at Fort Smith. From left to right are Nellie Mae (Barrow) Baird, Mary Louise (Stough) Seurlock, Leona (Marsh) Harrington, Harold Mott, Judson Greer, Virginia (Hawkins) Young, Margaret (Whittlesey) Clatterbuck, Harold Pinckney, and Margaret (Carpenter) Ladd. (Pebley Center, Boreham Library, University of Arkansas at Fort Smith.)

Ina Lee (Utley) Raymond and many others were baptized at Immanuel Baptist Church in 1937. Ina Raymond was the church secretary from 1946 to 1950. She lived with Lucy and G.A. Scott at 418 South Nineteenth Street in 1936–1937 when she moved from Paris, Arkansas. Lucy helped Ina's family find a home when they moved to Fort Smith. Ina later worked for Dyke Brothers Lumber from 1936 to 1946 and Southside Baptist Church from 1950 to 1982. (Fort Smith Museum of History.)

The Arkhola Sand and Gravel Company is pouring ready-mixed concrete at a construction site in the 1930s. The company operates at least three locations in Fort Smith and Van Buren today, contributing much to the local economy. (Fort Smith Museum of History.)

408 North C Street is seen in the 1940s. This photograph, taken by McCann Photographers, provides a slice of life of the working class in these neighborhoods. (McCann Collection, Fort Smith Museum of History.)

This Shotgun-type house at 304 North Fourth Street is an example of the economic diversity in Fort Smith. This photograph was part of a 1930s–1940s series taken by McCann Photography. (McCann Collection, Fort Smith Museum of History.)

Boy Scout Troop No. 24 is operating a radio exhibit and merit badge workshop, sponsored by Rotary International of Fort Smith, in the 1920s or 1930s. (Fort Smith Museum of History.)

Sgt. Marian Keck, winner of the 1936 Junior Music Club of Fort Smith, wrote to her former music teacher, Katherine Price Bailey, "from your favorite Sergeant." Keck has drawn in her new stripe as the photograph was taken before her promotion. Bailey would end her time as director of the Fort Smith Symphony in the 1940s due to so many of her students being "scattered by the war." (Bailey family collection.)

This 1936 McCann photograph shows the interior of Christ the King's Church on Greenwood Avenue and S Street, built in 1930. Robert E. McCann founded McCann Photography in the New Theatre Building on Garrison Avenue in 1918 and became one of the largest studios in the state by 1924. His son Robert E. McCann II was also a distinguished photographer who chronicled Fort Smith for decades. Their photographs are in the Fort Smith Museum of History. (McCann Collection, Fort Smith Museum of History.)

Christ the King's Church exterior, seen around 1949, was built in 1930 in the Spanish Mission Revival style. The building was damaged in a 1949 fire and restored soon after. It has received additional preservation in recent years. The church celebrated its 87th annual spring carnival on May 17–18, 2013. (Arthur Berry collection.)

This redbrick Massard School was built in 1930 and burned in 1936. The WPA rebuilt the school in 1937. The 1937 renamed Maness School structure was later used by German prisoners of war and remains on Wells Lake Road. According to Bud Patterson, "Massard was between Fort Smith and Barling on Highway 22, bounded by the river and Wildcat Mountain to the North; what is now Zero Street on the south; McNally Hill on the west, and what was then known as the Moody place on the East." The town grew from an 1820 land grant to William McAlister. After Camp Chaffee's 72,000 acres (including the community of Massard) were organized in the 1940s, 1,300 families were forced to leave, but the Maness School endured. (Ruth family collection.)

Here is a 1930s image of Immaculate Conception schoolchildren on the steps of their school. The names of some of the students are written on the photograph, but most are unidentified or illegible. Some names include Charley Young, Kelleam Greer, Fred Lumberg, Sophia Boteropolis, and Donald Burdyne. (Immaculate Conception School Archives.)

Melvina Fox, Laverne Sanders, and Maxine Fox are identified in this 1936 Ford. After graduating from Fort Smith High School in 1938, Sanders went on to serve as a radio operator (Wildcat Division) in World War II and was the fire chief of Fort Smith. Sanders retired as fire chief in 1972 and worked on church organs afterward. He was a member of Southside Baptist Church of Fort Smith. (Linoel Baker collection.)

Ida Lue (Turnipseed) Janes (left) gathers with her brother John W. "Bubba" Turnipseed and sister Lena Mae Catherine (Turnipseed) Giese in the 1940s near their grandparent's home, one of the oldest houses in the Choctaw Nation, which remains near Spiro, Oklahoma. Lena Mae married and later moved to Batavia, New York, where she lived until 2004, when she lost her battle with cancer. Her daughter Gina (Giese) Szczesny is a vice president with M&T Bank. John W. lives in northwest Arkansas and was an accountant for AT&T. He and his wife, Ruby, recently celebrated their 50th anniversary. They have two sons, William and Lt. Col. John Turnipseed. (Nick Janes and Maggie Janes Jones collection.)

Betty Jean (Baker) Mayberry, Ethel (Fox) Baker, and Bill John Baker holding Linoel Baker (born 1938) pose for a family picture around 1940. Bill's father, Edmund B. Baker, was a policeman for Fort Smith in the early 1900s. Bill worked for 47 years at Harding Glass, and Ethel was a poll worker. This photograph was taken near Edwards and Thirtieth or Thirty-first Streets. (Linoel Baker collection.)

Pictured are, from left to right, children Nanatta Sue (Casey) Bolin, R.D. Casey, and Bobby Randall Casey, and parents Flossie Lois Casey and Wesley Albert "Hoss" Casey. The Casey family lived at 2622 North Seventeenth Street. The Bois d'Arc trees are still in front of the homesite, but the house was removed in 2009. (R.D. Casey collection.)

Long Island Sandwich Shop in the 1930s on Garrison Avenue sold 10¢ hot dogs, hamburgers, and sandwiches. At the far right, a sign for the Palace Rooms is also visible. (Fort Smith Museum of History.)

A birthday party in the 1940s near the 2300 block of Ninth Street shows, from left to right, (first row) Larry Coleman, Gene Hartley, Danny Coleman, unidentified, Charlie Moss, Carolyn Burns, and two unidentified; (second row) Carl Harper, Bill Fox, unidentified, Linoel Baker, Donal Lunney, unidentified, Freddie Coleman, unidentified, Eddie Walker (University of Arkansas football alum), and Ronnie Burns. (Linoel Baker collection.)

1940s fishermen have pulled from the Arkansas River an alligator gar (approximately 180 to 200 pounds). Gars have been seen from Georgia to Nebraska but are declining in many areas. Some gator gar live 70 years and can be 10 feet long. John Stortz caught a similar gar in 2004 on the lower White River. Stortz's gar was eight feet long and weighed 240 pounds. (Fort Smith Museum of History.)

Goddard United Methodist Church at 1922 Dodson Avenue and Jenny Lind Road began as Dodson Avenue Methodist Episcopal Church in 1907, with "educational units" built in the 1920s. The current building was constructed in 1931 for $75,000. Additions to the church in the 1960s and 1990s contributed to its look today. It was renamed for Dr. O.E. Goddard, who steered the church through the Great Depression. (Fort Smith Museum of History.)

The boys of summer gather for a photograph around 1940 in Fort Smith. Baseball has had a long association with the area. The St. Louis Cardinals had a minor league team here, the major league Chicago White Sox and Pittsburgh Pirates once played an exhibition game at Andrews Field, and thousands of children have enjoyed summer and fall ball on Andrews Field, Hunts Park, and the Boys and Girls Clubs fields around Fort Smith for decades. (Robin Becker Morse and Bob Becker collection.)

The boys of summer become the boys of fall, as football is the game of choice in this photograph from the 1940s. Players are, from left to right, (first row) Charles Danley, Bobby Bell, Pat Garner, Cecil Russell, Dale Slaughter, Raymond Vaughn, and C.B. Turnipseed; (second row) Jerry Robinson, Bobby Joe Becker, Billy McGinnis, and Billy Vaughn. This photograph was taken behind Andrews Field. (Robin Becker Morse and Bob Becker collection.)

Franklin Jackman was a student of Katherine Price Bailey at the Southwestern Studios of Musical Art. He sent this picture to her during World War II. A marker at Oak Cemetery in Fort Smith reads that he served in the Coast Guard and was noted as lost at sea in 1943. (Bailey family collection.)

Fort Chaffee was originally created as Camp Chaffee on 72,000 acres in the early 1940s. Chaffee has been a military training facility for active and reserve personnel, a camp for German prisoners of war in the 1940s, Vietnamese refugees of the 1970s, and Cuban refugees who were processed through here in the 1980s. Victims of hurricane Katrina were also brought here in recent years. The area is seeing revitalization as parts of the former base are converted for housing, wildlife management areas, and industrial complexes. (Fort Smith Museum of History.)

John Robert Shipley is pictured in 1943 during World War II. Shipley had been a violin student at Southwestern Studios of Musical Art with his sister Sarah Ellen Shipley. John was in the Fort Smith Junior College class of 1941 and was a yearbook photographer and member of the band; he also served in the Marines. He died in Texas in 2001. (Bailey family collection.)

About 3,000 German prisoners of war were held at Camp Chaffee in July 1943. Much of their duty while in the camps dealt with conservation, farming, and construction. More than 23,000 German and Italian POWs were housed in Arkansas until 1946, when they were sent home to Europe. However, many of the prisoners of war eventually returned to the United States. (Pebley Center, Boreham Library, University of Arkansas at Fort Smith.)

Lewis Turner wrote on this photograph that he was "all set and rearin' to go to Chickasaw, Oklahoma." Turner trained at Chickasha Field with the AAF Central Flying Training Command of the 2549th Army Air Forces Base Unit. It is now a municipal airport. Turner had been a student at Southwestern Studios in Fort Smith. (Bailey family collection.)

"Marie's cab" was driven by the first female cab driver in Fort Smith, Marie V. (Eslinger) Mincher, from 1941 to 1949. Bob Staton, who owned the B&W Transfer Company, hired her originally. Marie's husband, John D. Mincher, was a manager at the company, and many women and elderly men were hired during World War II to drive the cabs. (Myrna Wells collection.)

The Fox family is seen in the 1940s near Kelley Highway in Fort Smith. Members are, from left to right, (first row) Lema (Fox) Coleman, "Mama" Melvina Fox, "Papa" Fred Fox, and Grace Fox (second row) Ethel Fox (Linoel Baker's mother), and Marietta Sutton; (third row) Jimmy Sutton, Irene Fox, Maxine Fox, Reba Fox, and Craig Sutton. Craig Sutton and son worked at Ward Furniture in Fort Smith for many years. Fred Fox had a long career at the Frisco Roundhouse and the post office. (Linoel Baker collection.)

Clarence Higgins (1917–1992) coached the 1946 American Legion baseball team; Higgins was also the director of the Fort Smith Boys Club from 1945 to 1971. "Hig" helped to build Hunts Park near Oak Cemetery in 1947 and was one of the founding fathers of Fort Smith Church League baseball in 1957. He established Babe Ruth Baseball in Arkansas and was a leader in American Legion baseball. He was inducted into the Babe Ruth Baseball Hall of Fame in 1987 and the Boys and Girls Club Hall of Fame in 1992. Additionally, he worked with St. Anne's high school football program at Hunts Park. (Billy Higgins collection.)

The Fort Smith Boys Club at 215 Wheeler Avenue was built in 1941 and served the community until 1980. The popular club Enter Ye Men of Tomorrow was located near B Street and Wheeler Avenue and is also about where the Sebastian County Detention Center is located now. Kids swam, played ball, and sometimes met celebrities such as *I Dream of Jeannie*'s Barbara Eden and "Cochise" Michael Ansara in the 1960s. (Billy Higgins collection.)

S.M. Hawkins (at left with glasses) assists a customer in his 901 Garrison Avenue pharmacy while a "beauty operator" does a Marcel at right around 1928. (Fort Smith Museum of History.)

The Fort Smith Municipal Airport, seen here in the 1950s, was established in 1939. Air transportation added a new dimension to the economy with a new terminal in the 1950s and the addition of the 188th Fighter Wing of the Air National Guard; Fort Smith Municipal Airport was the largest major city airport for hundreds of miles for decades. A new terminal was established in 2002. (Fort Smith Museum of History.)

This store was once at 501 Belle Avenue in Fort Smith. The image represents many neighborhood markets throughout Fort Smith that no longer exist, but at one time served a vital purpose to the citizens as they received groceries, gossip, and a connection with others there. (Fort Smith Museum of History.)

Billie J. (Turnipseed) Webb (left) and her cousin "Charlie Mack" Thurman have their portrait taken on June 18, 1949. Billie is the youngest daughter of William "Bill" and Maggie (Bowles) Turnipseed. Billie has been a secretary at Arkoma Elementary School since the 1960s, and her husband, Charles Webb, is a maintenance and custodial supervisor at Darby Junior High School in Fort Smith. Charlie was the son of Matthew and Lena Thurman. His sister Elizabeth lives in Fort Smith. (Billie Webb collection.)

Here, people enjoy the 1949 Christmas parade near Tenth Street and Garrison Avenue. Trolley lines and brick paving of earlier decades are visible. Harry "Happy" Russell Hestand (left in the car) was a master Mason of the Amrita Grotto within the Western Arkansas Scottish Rite Temple at 200 North Eleventh Street in Fort Smith. Hestand was mayor from 1952 to 1957. The Malco New Theatre, built in 1911 with funding from Fort Smith businessman George Sparks's will, is pictured with its 1920s and 1940s additions. The historic building still stands, while the Cisterna Fountain and Park currently occupy the space where the Army Store and Western Auto are in this photograph. (Caroline Speir collection.)

From left to right, children Larry, John, and Ed Ruth are at the Sharum Brothers store in Massard. S.T. "Bazz" Ruth later owned this store, which also served as the post office until rural farm delivery was organized in the area. This store was at Highway 22 near what is now Rogers Avenue and Massard Road in Fort Smith. (Ruth family collection.)

Frankie Ruth is seen on his ride to school from Ruth's Service Station in Massard. The Ruth family still lives in the area of Massard on Lee Street, which turns east off of Massard Road and "runs just about through the living room of my childhood home that my dad, granddad and uncles built," according to Rick Ruth. "The house was turquois with white trim." Rick's cousin Roger lives on the old homeplace on Massard Road. (Rick Ruth collection.)

This March 25, 1955, photograph of Fort Chaffee shows a portion of the 2,500 troops stationed there at that time, marching in review for Maj. Gen. Thomas Dunn, the installation's commanding general, and Fort Smith city officials, including Mayor Hestand. Hestand oversaw the renaming of Chaffee as a fort and the introduction of the 184th Tactical Reconnaissance Squadron, and brought Central Airlines to Fort Smith, which established St. Louis-to-Fort Smith flights. (Caroline Speir collection.)

Here, Mayor Hestand, Helen (Stoner) Hestand, and Jimmy Beckman send off Secretary of the Army Wilbur Brucker who visited Camp Chaffee. Brucker's March 1956 letter complimented Hestand on the "good will and cooperation . . . between Army personnel and the citizens of Fort Smith. . . . [Y]our efforts have contributed greatly to the admiration and respect which General Colbern and his troops have for you and your community." (Both, Caroline Speir collection.)

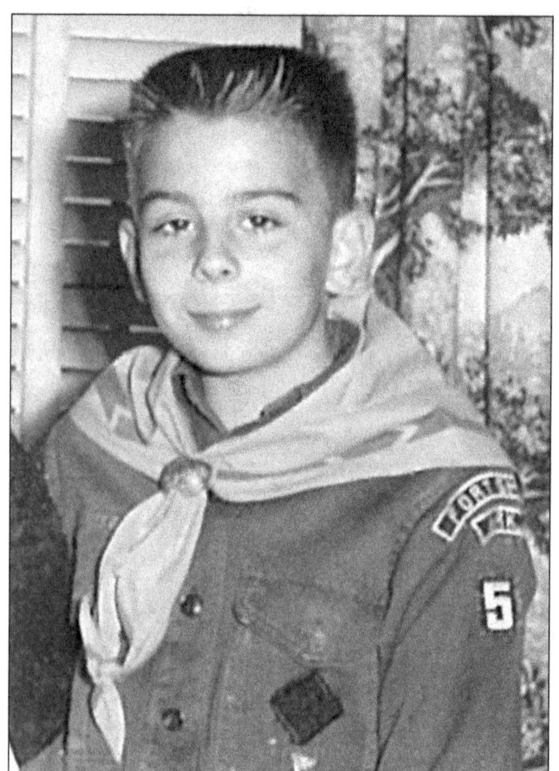

Dave Galloway is seen as a Cub Scout in Pack No. 5 of Fort Smith during the 1950s. Since then, Galloway has served on numerous Eagle boards of review in the area. He continues to encourage and teach hundreds of Scouts. Galloway assists with Scouting throughout the state. (Dave Galloway/Phillip and Andrew McClure collection.)

Linoel Baker's cousin Ronnie Burns stands alongside Linoel Baker's first car, a 1934 Ford, which Baker bought for $25. Linoel Baker always seemed to have a knack for tinkering. (Linoel Baker collection.)

Christ the King's Father Laughlin oversaw the construction of a rectory and Jewett Hall (the first school) in 1949. This new school (pictured) was built in 1954 for 122 students. By 1957, another addition was needed for the nearly 300 students. The current rectory was built in 1958, and a new church was added in 1972. The 1970s brought Vietnamese refugees to Fort Chaffee, and many of them continue to belong in the parish family. Christ the King is the ninth largest parish in the Diocese of Little Rock. (Arthur Berry collection.)

Children in the 1959–1960 kindergarten class are shown with the statue of Mary of the Immaculate Conception in the entrance of the Immaculate Conception School. This picture was taken on "free dress" day, meaning the students were to wear whatever they wanted for their class picture, which provides a time capsule of the fashions. (Immaculate Conception School Archives.)

Here, Jackie Brandt (left), who spent two years at Fort Chaffee, meets with Clarence Higgins, director of the Fort Smith Boys Club, and "Hal" Smith, the "Barling Darling" at Ronald Smith's home in Barling, Arkansas. Brandt hit .298 in the 1956 season before the Army, played 18 games in 1958, won a Gold Glove award in 1959, and was an All-Star in 1961. He played for the Cardinals, Giants, and Orioles. Harold Raymond Smith was a major league catcher from 1956 to 1961 for the Cardinals and in 1965 for the Pittsburgh Pirates. He was an All-Star in 1957 and 1959. He was also a minor league coach, manager, and scout for the Pirates, Reds, and Brewers. (Billy Higgins collection.)

Three

Life is Worth Living in Fort Smith and Worth Sharing

Ruth's Service Station in Massard, Arkansas, is pictured around 1955. It was near what is now Massard Road and Rogers Avenue in Fort Smith. The village of Massard was annexed by the city of Fort Smith after much of it became part of Fort Chaffee in the 1940s and 1950s. (Ruth family collection.)

Mose Smith Jr. started Smith Chevrolet in Fort Smith in 1938 when he bought Sutton Chevrolet at 105–115 North Seventeenth Street. Smith started selling Cadillacs in 1940. He died in 1983. (Brent McCord/Smith Chevrolet.)

Mose Smith's son John M. Smith started selling cars in 1959 and moved the dealership in 1963 to 1215 Highway 71 South (Zero Street as it turns to Towson Avenue). John M. added more brands to the Smith Auto Group, and the family continues to serve the river valley today through four generations. (Brent McCord/Smith Chevrolet.)

Bob Becker (left) and Adrian Jeffcoat show their trophies on Garrison Avenue around 1960. Becker was an athlete at St. Anne's in Fort Smith and on local semiprofessional baseball teams. He started Becko Machine Works at 1000 Dodson Avenue. (Robin Becker Morse and Bob Becker collection.)

The 1954–1955 Immaculate Conception Junior High School football team is pictured. Seventh-through ninth-grade students would move from Immaculate Conception to Trinity Junior High School in 1986. (Immaculate Conception School Archives.)

The 1954–1955 Immaculate Conception School cheerleading squad included, from left to right, Barbara Hug, Holly Corrotto, Mary Margaret Harper, Elaine McKenzie, Sandra Crabtree, Mary Catherine Moellers, Carole Udouj, and Suzanne Murta. (Immaculate Conception School Archives.)

The 1955–1956 fifth-grade students are on the steps of Immaculate Conception School. Notice the Cub Scout uniforms, class T-shirts, and rolled jeans. Some things never change as students today at this school are still often seen attending Cub Scout meetings or wearing a class T-shirt on special days, and some still roll their jeans. (Immaculate Conception School Archives.)

Larry Coleman and his cousin Linoel Baker (right) are pictured in 1953–1954. Coleman had a Mustang. Baker bought the Allstate cycle at Sears on Garrison. Baker would later own Universal Joint Specialists Inc. at 1909 Towson Avenue from 1975 to 2003. Baker's business involved complete driveshaft repair and general mechanic work. (Linoel Baker collection.)

Ida Lue (Turnipseed) and James Loren Janes were married at Fort Chaffee after his stint in the US Army, serving as artillery, supply, and playing baseball. He also did some accounting on the side. A native of Farber, Missouri, "Jimmy" met Ida Lue in Fort Smith. Ida Lue was working at the Boston Store when this photograph was taken on August 25, 1956, at their reception in the home of Roy and Irene Huffman. (Nick Janes and Maggie Janes Jones collection.)

This 1950s view of Garrison Avenue shows a Christmas float from Immaculate Conception School, Franklin's, Kinney Shoes, and the Boston Store. (Immaculate Conception School Archives.)

Constantino's at 407 Garrison Avenue served spaghetti and meatballs and barbecued ribs and beer. It was a favorite gathering place on Sunday afternoons in the 1930s, 1940s, and 1950s, according to Arthur Berry. The original owners were Antonio Constantino, who was born in Turin, Italy, in 1870 and died in Fort Smith in 1922, and Francisca Constantino, who was born in Rivarolo, Italy, in 1872 and died in Fort Smith in 1955. The restaurant changed hands and closed by the 1970s. (Arthur Berry collection.)

Randall Ford evolved from its 1908 beginnings to this location (12–24 North Eleventh Street) in Fort Smith by 1953. Many Fort-Smithers recall this location from the 1950s and 1960s. (Bradford Randall collection.)

In the 1950s, Garrison Avenue was packed with shops of all kinds, soldiers, salesmen, business people, tourists, and families; it was the center of everything. The 1960s and 1970s would see a dramatic shift as urban sprawl, cheap motels, and inflation killed downtowns across America. (Fort Smith Museum of History.)

Billie G. Neisler, mother of Lisa Neisler (a 1986 Southside High School graduate), is shown here walking down the south side of Garrison Avenue toward the river around 1937. Jason Don Neisler, Billie's husband, worked at Dixie Cup in Fort Smith for many years. (Lisa Neisler collection.)

Here is the 1961–1963 vocal music class of Katherine Price Bailey, who lived to be 102 and continued to teach music and publish poetry after she retired. Her influence is felt through the numerous students she taught, the friends she taught with, and the organization she and her husband started, the Fort Smith Symphony. (Bailey family collection.)

Mary Frances Cooley is shown at her fragrance and candy counter in this 1960s photograph of her family's pharmacy at 128 North Greenwood Avenue in Fort Smith. (Fort Smith Museum of History.)

Wade (far right) and Mary Frances Cooley (far left) meet with a representative from the King Candy Company and a customer in the 1960s. Cooley's Pharmacy was at 128 North Greenwood Avenue in Fort Smith. (Fort Smith Museum of History.)

The Fort Smith Automotive Smokers (named for the coffin factory smelter near their field at Zero and South Thirty-first Streets) played from 1949 to 1958 and dominated the state's thriving semi-pro baseball league, winning state titles in 1954, 1957, and 1958, according to the *Southwest Times Record*. The team won five districts and played in five semiprofessional national championships. The team reunited in 1999. Members are, from left to right, (first row) batboys Randy Robinson and C.B. Wright; (second row) Billy "Ears" McGinnis, Bob Becker, Harold Bateman, Cecil Horn, Cy Perkins, E.J. Sellars, and C.B. Turnipseed; (third row) Alton Robinson, Paul Rout, and George Becker. (Both, Bob Becker collection.)

This is the Paul Lewis Orchestra on April 2, 1962, at the Cosmetologist Dance at the Holiday Inn in Fort Smith. This band played for over 18 years at the Billy Garner Supper Club, the Order of United Commercial Travelers Club, Dervish Club, and Century Club. The main band members were Paul Lewis, Dorothy Gibson, Paul Flippen, James Shoffey, Herbie Echols (who played with Dean Martin), and Foster Merk. Various others included Marion Mondier, George Hunt, and Bob Land. (Fort Smith Museum of History.)

Southside High School on Gary Street in Fort Smith was dedicated in 1963. The first class had 282 graduates. Victor E. Stewart was the principal for 19 years. Wayne Haver has been the principal since. Present enrollment is at 1,573. Larry Loux taught history at Southside for 38 years, while former Fort Smith mayor C. Ray Baker taught history there for 44 years. Northside and Southside High Schools annually have some of the top academic and extracurricular students in the state and in the nation. (Pebley Center, Boreham Library, University of Arkansas at Fort Smith.)

Here is the Creekmore Pool at Creekmore Park during the summer of 1964. The original park opened in the 1940s and remains a special place for many. The pool is home to the Fort Smith Tideriders and Arkansas Masters Swimming, and is also available to the general public. The pool and splashpad are open all summer. (Fort Smith Museum of History.)

Clyde Randall Jr. is pictured with the new driver training car at the new Rogers Avenue location of Randall Ford in 1967. Randall Ford is a fourth-generation dealership in Fort Smith. (Bradford Randall collection.)

Linoel Baker served in the Arkansas Air National Guard as a fireman from 1961 to 1967. Many members of his family were members of Fort Smith Fire Department or volunteers. Baker was also a mechanic and local businessman in Fort Smith for many years. He has three daughters, LeeAnn, Diana, and Jennifer. (Linoel Baker collection.)

Ramsey Junior High in Fort Smith currently has 925 students. Ramsey, Chaffin, Kimmons, and Darby are the public junior high schools in Fort Smith. Ramsey is a fixture of the old "Southtown" of Fort Smith, which expanded from downtown in the 1960s to annex this area and to the west. Ramsey offers career- and college-readiness curriculums and overall excellent academic and extracurricular programs. (Pebley Center, Boreham Library, University of Arkansas at Fort Smith.)

Kimmons Junior High is a major partner with the University of Arkansas at Fort Smith and the surrounding neighborhood. Most recently, students worked at University of Arkansas at Fort Smith with the Women's Foundation of Arkansas to help students plan for the future. Additionally, the school fields strong music programs, offers free tutoring in mathematics and other subjects, and has been recognized by the governor for excellence in technology and other career fields. (Pebley Center, Boreham Library, University of Arkansas at Fort Smith.)

Clarence "Hig" Higgins is third from right as a member of the state's first Educational Television Commission. Higgins operated the Oark General Store and farmed as well as serving as director of the Fort Smith Boys Club for many years. Billy D. Higgins, son of Clarence and Opal Higgins, is an associate professor of history at University of Arkansas at Fort Smith and the author of many articles and two books, *A Stranger and a Sojourner: Peter Caulder, Free Black Frontiersman in Antebellum Arkansas* (2004) and *The Barling Darling: Hal Smith in American Baseball* (2009). (Billy D. Higgins collection.)

Pettus Kincannon (first row, left), with Raymond James, works for the Center for Lifelong Learning at the University of Arkansas at Fort Smith as a certified financial planner. Most importantly, he has worked with Troop No. 110 in Fort Smith. He is pictured here with six other local boys earning their Eagle in 1965. He is a Northside High School graduate and an alum of the University of Arkansas at Fayetteville. (Pettus Kincannon/Phillip and Andrew McClure collection.)

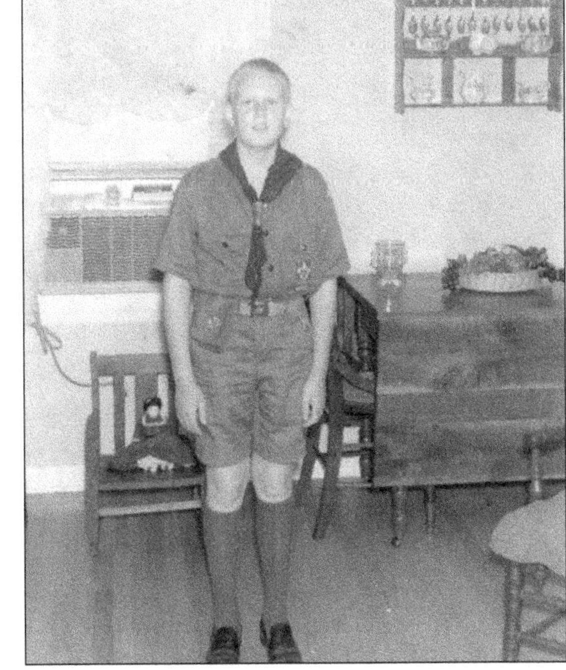

John Spain, a local engineer at Ingersoll Rand in Fort Smith, is shown in his Boy Scout uniform in the 1960s. Spain is a volunteer at the Fort Smith National Historic Site and has recently offered workshops about the music of the Civil War and spoken about Deputy US Marshal Heck Thomas. (John Spain/Phillip and Andrew McClure collection.)

Shelby Breedlove (left), the third president of Fort Smith Junior College, is seen working a table at the Arkansas-Oklahoma State Fair for the Community College Enabling Act, which would help Fort Smith Junior College to become Westark Junior College in 1966. These grassroots efforts and Amendment 52 to the Arkansas State Constitution in 1964, which allowed two-year colleges to receive public funding, helped the institution and the area economy grow. (Pebley Center, Boreham Library, University of Arkansas at Fort Smith.)

In 1950–1952, Fort Smith Junior College moved from what is now Northside High School to Grand Avenue to become a two-year college. The first nine graduates in 1930 had attended classes at what is now Darby Junior High and, at times, under the football stadium at Northside High School. In the 1960s, Fort Smith Junior College existed on 40 acres off of Grand and Waldron Avenues. "Old Main," as this building was once known, was constructed when the college moved to Grand Avenue but was demolished in 1967–1968. (Pebley Center, Boreham Library, University of Arkansas at Fort Smith.)

The Vines Building, located behind the footprint of Old Main, evolved with the expansion of Westark Junior College (1965–1973), Westark Community College (1973–1998), Westark College (1998–2001), and today's University of Arkansas at Fort Smith (2002 to present). This building has served as an administration building, classroom space, and offices. (Pebley Center, Boreham Library, University of Arkansas at Fort Smith.)

Hundreds of people have been taught in Shelia Croxton's studio on Greenwood Avenue since 1977. Croxton continues to teach her piano method class here. Croxton began teaching in August 1961 at Jenkins Music Store on Garrison Avenue as part of her University of Arkansas requirements. She earned a bachelor's of music, bachelor's of science in music education, and a master's in music education. She taught public school in Fayetteville for 16 years. Her son Kevin, who began playing the piano at age four and a half in her class, teaches at Van Buren Public Schools and composes music for commercials, documentary films, and movies. He has received numerous Telly Awards, Addy awards, Axiom Awards, and an Emmy for a documentary in 2009. He also wrote the score for the film *Typanum*. (Shelia Croxton collection.)

Andy Caperton (left) grew up in Greenwood, Arkansas, earned his Eagle in 1978, and later used the skills he learned in missions in the Andes Mountains and on the Amazon River. (Andy Caperton/Phillip and Andrew McClure collection.)

At center is George E. "Chip" Marrin, Scoutmaster for Troop No. 380 in Fort Smith, during a 1973 campout near Pine Bluff, Arkansas. Marrin is a dedicated Scoutmaster and a volunteer for various district and council activities. He devotes himself to the Scouting program, his wife, Judy, and their son, Alex. (Chip Marrin/Phillip and Andrew McClure collection.)

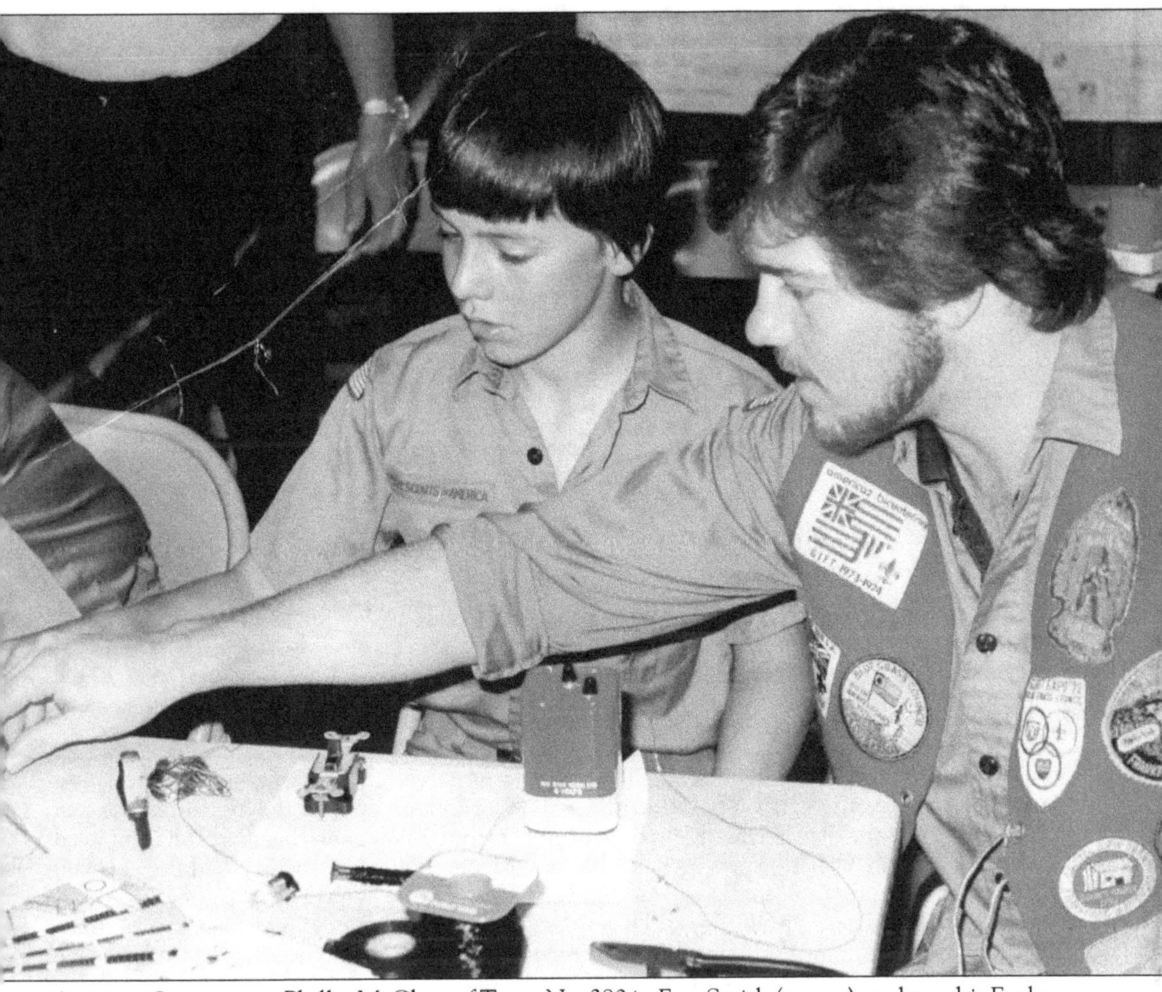

Assistant Scoutmaster Phillip McClure of Troop No. 380 in Fort Smith (center) works on his Eagle project around 1977. McClure's son Andrew is one of the youngest Eagle Scouts in Fort Smith. Andrew McClure's work can be seen at the Fort Smith Museum of History. Phillip McClure is the pastor of River Valley Christian Church. (Phillip McClure collection.)

Reed's Twin Burger Drive-in at 2400 Tulsa Street (as it curves off of Twenty-fourth Street) is a neighborhood favorite. Owned by Delbert Michael Wipf and run by Wipf and his mother, Alvetta "Al," it began as the Slaeden family's two-room grocery in the 1940s and then Earl and Lena Reed opened a drive-in. Other owners included Leo and Marge Byrum and then Harold Parrish, who "had a bad morning" and sold it to Jack and Kaye French. The Wipfs purchased it in 2005. Al says that every owner "wishes they still had it;" she also says the place is "old, but Clorox clean." Gayle Burton, who ran World Burger for Mr. Yocum, is cooking hamburgers the same now as she did at World Burger all those years ago. The hamburger stand is a dying breed, but one worth saving and worth sharing. (Author's collection.)

The Janes family is seen about 1970. After Fort Chaffee and graduating from Northeastern Missouri State University (now Truman State) in Kirksville, James Loren Janes (top left) returned to Fort Smith in the 1960s and worked for Jimmy Taylor, the Farmer's Co-Op in Van Buren, Whirpool, and Plastics Research and Development Co. He started a successful screen-printing business at 1914 South S Street in Fort Smith. Around that time, he also established Loren Janes Tax and Accounting there, which he still operates today. He and his daughter, Maggie (Janes) Jones (bottom right), are dealers for Drake Income Tax Software in five states. Nick Janes (bottom left) is a computer engineer in Tucson, Arizona, where he resides with his wife, Kim. James Loren Janes's wife, Ida Lue (Turnipseed) Janes (top right), inspired the research for Arcadia Publishing's Postcard History Series: *Fort Smith* with her humorous stories of living in the area. She passed away in Fort Smith on November 20, 2012, at age 77. (Nick Janes and Maggie Janes Jones collection.)

www.ingramcontent.com/pod-product-compliance
Lightning Source LLC
LaVergne TN
LVHW081542100826
845153LV00004B/290

* 9 7 8 1 5 3 1 6 6 8 5 5 6 *